1987 $4—

7/19/18

NORTHWEST VARIETY

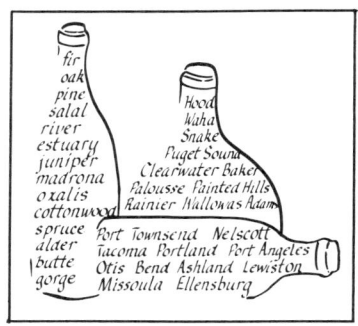

NORTHWEST VARIETY:
Personal Essays
By 14 Regional Authors

Edited By
Lex Runciman
and Steven Sher

Arrowood Books, Inc.

Copyright 1987 by Arrowood Books, Inc.

No portion of this book may be reprinted or republished in any form without the express written permission of the author.

Acknowledgments:

"New to the Country," by William Kittredge, originally appeared in *Montana: The Magazine of Western History*, Vol. 36, No. 1. Copyright 1986 by William Kittredge. Reprinted by permission.

"My Father's Love Letters," by Tess Gallagher, was published in *A Concert of Tenses: Essays on Poetry*, by Tess Gallagher. Ann Arbor: The University of Michigan Press, 1986. Previously published in *American Poetry Review* 10, No. 3 (1981). Copyright 1981 by Tess Gallagher. Reprinted by permission.

"Confessions of 'An Oregon Playwright'," by Charles Deemer, first appeared in *Oregon English*, Fall/Winter 1986. Copyright 1986 by Charles Deemer. Reprinted by permission.

"Our Linoleum Age," by Paul Pintarich, first appeared in *The Oregonian — Northwest Magazine*, Sept. 21, 1986. Copyright 1986 by the Oregonian Publishing Co. Reprinted by permission.

Typeset at Arrowood Books and the Franklin Press, Seattle, Washington. Printed in the U.S.A. by McNaughton & Gunn, Ann Arbor, Michigan.

This book is printed on acid-free paper.

First Edition

Published by Arrowood Books, Inc., P.O. Box 2100, Corvallis, Oregon 97339

Library of Congress Cataloging-in-Publication Data

Northwest variety.

    Bibliography: p.146
    1. American literature—Northwestern States—History and criticism. 2. American literature—20th century—History and criticism. 3. Northwestern States—Intellectual life. 4. Northwestern States in literature. 5. Regionalism in literature. 6. Authorship.

I. Runciman, Lex.   II. Sher, Steven.

PS282.N67   1987   810'.9'9795   86-28876

ISBN 0-934847-04-5 (alk. paper)
ISBN 0-934847-05-3 (pbk. : alk. paper)

Contents

Preface . . . .*vi*
Introduction . . . .*viii*

Mark Halperin, "No One Quite Trusts the Weather:
                Writing in the Northwest" 12
Vern Rutsala, "The Frozen Lake" 20
Tess Gallagher, "My Father's Love Letters" 30
Paul Pintarich, "Our Linoleum Age" 46
Vi Gale, "The Negotiating Eye:
                Is There a Northwest Outlook?" 52
Richard Hoyt, "Distilled in Oregon" 58
M. K. Wren, "Out of Amarillo" 66
William Kittredge, "New to the Country" 72
Laura Jensen, "Stars and Streetlights" 86
Charles Deemer, "Confessions of 'An Oregon Playwright'" . . .94
Lawson Fusao Inada, "Living in the Northwest" 104
Madeline DeFrees, "Sea-Fever: The Subjective
                Geography of the Poem" 114
Sam Hamill, "Here and Now" 126
Robert Wrigley, "The Swing, the Snow,
                the Skull of a Hare" 138

Authors' Works 146

Preface

In editing this book, our aim has been to bring together the comments, views, and reflections of a range of successful Northwest writers, asking each to speak of his or her relationship to this part of the country. Such a book, we thought, ought to provide good reading (the best sort of advertising for its contributors), and we hoped such a book might, by the range of its responses, suggest the complexity of what is often loosely referred to as "a sense of place."

As we thought about the authors we might approach, several criteria helped us make decisions. These writers, we decided, had to be current Northwest residents. They had to be successful, having published the equivalent of three (or more) books. And taken together, we wished them to represent as broad a mix of writers as we could get. That meant looking for geographical diversity—within Oregon, Washington, Idaho, and Western Montana—and it meant looking for participation by both popular and literary writers. Several writers we contacted wished us well, but were already heavily scheduled. A few never answered our letters at all. The final selection here is, we feel, a strong and worthy assemblage, and we're happy to stand behind it. It is also true that two or even three other such volumes could (at least theoretically) be compiled without exhausting the pool of remarkable Northwest talent.

This book is also in its small way a benefit for the Richard Hugo Memorial Scholarship Fund at the University of Montana. Hugo, who died in 1982, was a much-loved teacher, and his work remains an influential and distinctive American voice. Twelve percent of the purchase price of each copy of *Northwest Variety* sold is pledged to the Hugo Scholarship Fund, to benefit student writers enrolled in the University of Montana's graduate writing program.

Northwest Variety has been a truly collaborative undertaking. Special thanks are due first to the authors whose work is here presented. They responded warmly and wholeheartedly to a project which asked much of them, with no return other than publication itself, and contributions made to the Richard Hugo Memorial

Scholarship Fund. That this book exists at all is a tribute to their characters, to their affection for this region as well as for Dick Hugo and his work, and to their interest in helping generate even modest scholarship funds for student writers.

Thanks also to Washington state arts administrator Lee Bassett, for originally conceiving the idea of a benefit book, and to Prof. Lois Welch, Hugo Scholarship Committee member, for her encouragement.

A host of others helped out or provided encouraging words: our thanks to William Stafford, Jean Auel, Ivan Doig, Ken Kesey, Barry Lopez, Patrick McManus, Eve Triem, Sharon Woods, Jo Alexander, Jeff Grass, and Robert Frank. Thanks to colleague Lisa Ede for her interest and encouragement. Thanks to Nancy Sher for her support, as well as for early suggestions regarding cover design. Thanks to Carol Williams for her art. And special thanks to Debbie Runciman, who keyboarded, coded, and proofed a good portion of this text, and who has acted as a trusted and respected sounding board on all manner of concerns, editorial and otherwise.

Introduction

In June of 1846, a treaty between Great Britain and the U.S. ended years of simmering political debate over what was then called the Oregon Country. Two years later, the Oregon Territory was formed, incorporating what are now the states of Idaho, Washington, and Oregon, as well as portions of Montana and Wyoming. At about that same time, Henry David Thoreau was drafting an account of his time in a small cabin on a Massachussetts pond. Published in 1854, *Walden's* concluding chapter is a passionate mix of exhortation, exclamation, and rhetorical inquiry, including these lines: "–what does the West stand for? Is not our own interior white on the chart?"

What the Northwest "stands for" continues to be a topic of lively discussion. As editors, we thought it both fitting and interesting to ask Northwest writers what this area means to them, as individuals, and especially as working writers. In short, we asked them, "Why live, work, and write *here*?" Their answers, as various as the landscapes of this region, make up this book.

Many of these writers are Northwest natives, born and raised in towns like Port Angeles, McCall, Hillsboro, or Hermiston, as well as in cities like Tacoma or Portland. Others have come here from elsewhere–Fresno, or Amarillo, or Pasadena. They live now in college or mill towns (Ashland, Lewiston, Missoula, Ellensburg), in large metropolitan areas (Seattle, Tacoma, Portland), and in places in between (Port Townsend, Land's End). All of these writers publish regularly; a bibliography of their works is included following the last essay. They write poems, stories, mysteries, translations, thrillers, screenplays, comedies, criticism, and drama; and their books have been translated into Italian, German, French, and Dutch. Of the fourteen essays presented here, twelve were penned by their authors especially for this book. Two essays, those by Tess Gallagher and William Kittredge, are reprinted with grateful permission. Written with this book in mind, several other essays have also seen magazine publication.

And what *does* the West, the Northwest, stand for? "Absence as much as presence" (Mark Halperin). "A stage even before I begin to write" (Charles Deemer). "The influence of Pacific Rim nations" (Vi Gale). "Rainforests . . . the High Desert lying in the rain shadow of the Cascades, and the stark, lean Basin and Range country" (M. K. Wren). "Farmers and loggers and wastrels, friends and enemies, the people of the Northwest who, for better or worse, made up the population that counted for me" (Vern Rutsala). And "one of the most hideous products of mankind—the Trident nuclear submarine base at Bangor" (Sam Hamill). As these essays reveal, the Northwest is more than its physical landscape: tule marshes and sagebrush flats, sand barchans, downtown Seattle and Old Tacoma, Warner Rim, a working parade of ships in and out of the Straits of San Juan de Fuca. It is also, as Madeline DeFrees suggests, our "subjective geography."

Some of the essays in this book stay within fairly narrow personal boundaries. They remember individuals, and the times those individuals made real. They recreate specific locales. They map personal changes and determine what those changes mean. Other essays speak consciously and directly to larger concerns. They speak of our roles as Northwest citizens. They address political, ecological, cultural, philosophical, even religious issues. There is humor in these pages, and erudition, and much humane reflection.

"We are acquainted with a mere pellicle of the globe on which we live . . . We know not where we are." Thoreau, ever the master of multiple meanings, may well have been right and continue to be right. But he would also have been the last person to suggest that our effort to know is useless or without recompense. We have found these essays to be often fascinating personal documents by some representatives of the Northwest's richly diverse writing community. It is these writers' business to entertain, provoke, stimulate, and indulge our need to explore who and where we are. We believe, as we hope you will, that here they admirably succeed.

Lex Runciman
Steven Sher
Corvallis, Oregon

NORTHWEST VARIETY

Mark Halperin

MARK HALPERIN is a New York native. He graduated with a degree in physics from Bard College, worked for a time as a research physicist, and later as an electron microscope technician. A graduate of the Iowa Writers Workshop, Halperin moved to Ellensburg, Washington in 1966, where he continues to teach at Central Washington University. He has published several collections of poetry, most recently *A Place Made Fast*, from Copper Canyon Press. He is currently spending a year in Japan.

No One Quite
Trusts the Weather:
Writing in the Northwest

The room I sit in has a large window through which I look out, as I have for many years now, at a scene that never fails to draw me. Close by is a young apple tree. Perhaps it is stunted. It seems the same small, twisted, scruffy tree I bought on sale years ago. Further out, a swamp begins, with willows that are yellow-tipped and magenta. There's snow on the ground but later, when spring comes and the ditch on the hill that ends the swamp is running with water—its seepage makes the swamp—a curtain of green will appear. Atop the first rise a solitary pine waves in the famous Ellensburg wind. I've seen I don't know how many hawks—redtails and marshhawks primarily, but there must have been others—scan the land for food from its top. And further back there's only sagebrush, rise after rise to the last. For a month at most there will be masses of lupine and balsam root. When that burns off, the brown will be unrelieved.

* * *

I walk there and look for stones, Ellensburg Blues (agates), though mostly in the fall and spring. I suspect rattlesnakes in the summer when it's often too hot for long walks anyway. In the winter, if the snow's deep enough to cover the rock and sagebrush, my family and I cross-country ski there. We've seen muledeer dot the ridge, and with the wind in our faces, skied almost up to them. Several really cold winters we've watched elk come down those deer trails.

* * *

Even now I can see the first change that will come. Snow's gone. The muddy brown is settling in. Yellowstarts spread across the fields, then monkshood—all the flowers; I will have forgotten their names and will have to look them up.

* * *

Is that the Northwest? It's a puzzle. Tomorrow I will be reading about Lafcadio Hearne. Maybe I will find something I want to pursue by writing about it. Or maybe his life will touch mine somewhere close enough to get me writing. Though it will be Japan, Matsue, I put into the poem or into my imagining of the situation, I will look up so often that something of this scene will come in too.

* * *

When I think of what I've written, I recognize a landscape filled with hills and the river which I visit almost daily. The shimmering of aspens appears because I live within their limbs and soft, oozing scars. Trout and an occasional river otter break the surface. There is a calm that is easy to enter.

* * *

I know that is only a rural landscape. Yet its four seasons locate it outside the South and Southwest, the closeness of mountains outside the Midwest as does the smell of salt water which I can drive to in two hours. There is no particular ethos I recognize, no deep-seated tradition to contact. That may be for the best too. I have enough connections of that sort, heritages, not to want more. I begin to wonder if that isn't part of what this place is for me, absence as much as presence.

* * *

Aside from the few here, writers are people I don't see frequently. The best known poet in the region is William Stafford. I wonder if I would ever have met him if I hadn't lived here—not because he would be hard to approach (I can't think of anyone easier)—but because I find it hard. Here our paths cross; we say things that must last until the next time. I feel the same way about Vern Rutsala, about others. Do people with more fiercely ambitious natures go East or South? If Northwest writers are not "laid back," they like to pretend they are.

* * *

Although "Northwest" suggests "rainy," only the coastal area is. The prevalent weather here is wind. Everyone walks slightly bent over from bucking it. If that exaggerates, you *can* read the normal wind direction by looking at a grove of trees: the side that meets the brunt of the oncoming rush of air is lower. Wind becomes another voice you can't quite understand, mumbling on the side of the house, in the chimney.

* * *

My family and I traveled to Mt. Hood to ski and visit a friend. A mountain can dominate a view, a mind, imposing by controlling the perspective. The weekend was clear, too warm really to ski and too clear not to. So we did, then drove home by way of the Columbia Gorge, marveling at the scenery both there and back. People in Alaska must do that and in Vermont maybe. Maybe they do in all parts of the country and maybe everywhere is as lovely as this, but I'm not taking chances. Being a Northwest writer is being a partisan to this landscape as much as anything else, failing to understand the allegiances of others.

* * *

Doodling like this has reminded me of Auden's "In Praise of Limestone." If I could choose to admire only one quality of Auden's it would be his moral consciousness. The sweep of his mind, his firm grounding in literature are beyond me and, because of that, foreign. But his moral outlook, as exemplified in that poem, is within my understanding. I recall a party I went to on the other side of the valley. It was late spring, afternoon. Guests were milling around drinking wine and making small talk. We could see the Cascades, among them Mt. Stuart, the snow-covered tallest peak in a granite subrange named after it. The air had a clarity and nip that encouraged an extra glass or two. A man I hardly knew asked how I would write about that view that stretched glinting before us. Before I had thought much, I said, "I'd put a person in it." I would too, though now I think I would fall back on all I knew of that landscape, the hikes I'd taken, the history I'd read, my sense of its fish and game. Auden has it both ways: he totally involves us in the scene, peopling it, and then reminding us he is speaking to someone. That's when he moralizes the landscape:

>   . . . but when I try to imagine a faultless love
>   Or the life to come, what I hear is the murmur
>   Of underground streams, what I see is a limestone landscape.

I can only think how lost I would feel without this landscape, how it has become home to me as the place I wish to be.

* * *

The snow has actually melted, the first warmth of spring arrived. It's been like this for better than a week and no one quite trusts the weather. We're all weary of winter, but this seems too sudden. What happened to thirty and forty degree temperatures? Spring is blowing in and there's no getting around the wind. In the view from my window, white has been replaced by gray-brown. The sheaths and stalks of last year's grasses are a matting. Hints of green show up here and there, though not well yet. The poplars haven't produced catkins. At most there are new calves and ranchers happy that the early spring makes their tasks easier.

* * *

People talk to me about gardening, one of those topics that cuts across all social bounds. We have a short but not impossible season for tomatoes, peppers, even melons. Planting—when's too early, when's too late—are subjects of great and grave debate. Which varieties, which methods—once we flush all the greenthumbs out, once the hardware stores and nurseries start reporting roses, it will be hard for people like me, with divided loyalties, to keep inside. To live here is to be outdoors. Otherwise a city would be better, a real city where you have little sense of landscape. Seattle, our city by adoption, hardly qualifies since you can see two mountain ranges on the rare, clear day—Olympics to the west and Cascades this way.

* * *

To be a writer or serious artist of any sort requires major adjustments when you live in a rural area. But if you live in Seattle or Portland you're apt to feel "out of the way" or cut off. If you need a sense of society, you are apt to be constantly frustrated. If you need to be close to a pulse, I think you feel abandoned as well. If that's not the case, though, you can gain an enlarged perspective. Here writing can only be part of a life, I think—a big part, the biggest, but never the entire thing. If it is, you ought to be in New York or Chicago or Los Angeles or San Francisco. There will never be enough people who will understand here, and if you have no other way to make contact with people, your suffering will be endless. And needless.

* * *

For most writers, attempting writers, failure is a natural condition. We do not succeed in writing what we had intended – not as much, not as fully. We do not get what we do write published as often as we want, in the places we want – nor is it read by as many people or as closely as we had hoped. Should it be? For most of us it's hard to answer yes. In the nature of this enterprise more people must want to write than can, than could succeed, than the world has need or use for. What I have to learn again and again and what my rural landscape teaches me is to remember: *you must write for yourself, that is your natural audience and condition*. It is very hard to accept that. It takes a big landscape with lots of rabbits, a place dogs can run . . . There are no places that make it easy; this one makes it possible.

* * *

Writer, poet, Northwest or regional or Deep Image or Jewish or . . . Someone refused permission to include his work in an anthology that represented more than his "sort" of writing. I was dismayed reading that in an introduction. Shouldn't art, of all activities, promote diversity – isn't that our richness? Yet I know how much easier it is for me to start one work than another. I make a simple, unconscious identification that brushes past introductions when I see the name of a place I know in a poem, or recognize one of my concerns. It's so obvious that Americans will find it easier than non-Americans to respond to a piece by a fellow countryman of the same generation and social experience that I forget it. If I want to read Wyatt, why not? If Gilgamesh is a favorite or I respond deeply to Lampkin, none of that disproves my initial observation. Being a Northwest writer is admitting that I pick up my ears when I hear about Mt. St. Helens or Bangor, that I can choose to respond to the stories of the Yakimas as partially mine.

* * *

Spring is here. I keep poking around in the aspen leaves looking for morels. The swamp has come alive, not with color yet, but with waves of choral episodes at night. Owls are hooting, coyotes cackling in the distance. Each morning I hear meadowlarks whistle from small hills and low branches. One of my dogs, the dark one, is a bee catcher. I watch her jump into the air; I listen for her howls of success. The other dog is a rooter for moles, leaper over sagebrush. She makes mad dashes "for the fun of it." I had forgotten spring includes looking at the river to see if it's gone up or down, gotten clearer or more muddied. Here, this writer fits his writing in after checking the weather report.

Vern Rutsala

Photo by Joan Rutsala

VERN RUTSALA was born in McCall, Idaho, and moved to Portland at the age of eight. He graduated from Reed College in 1956, served in the Army, then went back to school, graduating from the Iowa Writers Workshop in 1960. Since 1961, he has taught at Lewis and Clark College in Portland, with visiting appointments at the University of Minnesota and Bowling Green State University. A sabbatical and a Guggenheim Fellowship allowed him to spend two separate years living in London. He has also been awarded two fellowships from the National Endowment for the Arts. His eleventh book, *Ruined Cities*, was recently published by Carnegie-Mellon University Press.

The Frozen Lake

Once, years ago, when I was flying west, I looked out the window of the plane and was sure I saw the area in Idaho where I was born. It was December and the landscape below looked frozen but I was certain I recognized every feature – the lake, the small town scattered along its edge, the mountain presiding over it all, and a finger-like valley. It all lay there stiffly in place, utterly frozen, as the plane moved along and at that moment, feeling the oddity and curiosity of it all, I wanted to slow the plane down so that I could keep looking. Out of all the vast scenes below I had happened to look down to see the one I should see. Some part of me went down to that snow-dusted landscape as if trying to thaw it back to life – an effort made in many poems since then – and part of me drew back, seeing the scene like a relief map caught in the deep freeze of lost time. I remembered the old summer vividness of the area but now there was something nearly prehistoric about it. Then of course it faded as the plane plowed toward Portland.

That scene came back to me often but found its way into only one small poem which seemed inadequate. But the image remained and kept surfacing from time to time in a nagging way. It seemed to represent the inaccessibility of the past and in particular what was my deepest experience of the Northwest. I had lived in the Northwest much of my life and its atmosphere was in my work as well as the tone of the region, but I had only confronted some of my earliest experiences in oblique ways with images here and there – an unfinished barn, a bobcat thumping down on pine needles, a sense of trees and shadows. It occurred to me that we may live in a place but living there doesn't mean we have a vital access to it. Key experiences may be buried and the process of discovery means chipping away and dredging or even melting. Now this is easier said than done, of course. But that image of the frozen lake remained and kept nudging its way into my notebooks. By fits and starts it also began to become clear that for me the Northwest was in large part a whole collection of stories and images lodged in the past, possibly locked in that frozen lake. There had to be a way of unlocking it.

The reason I was flying to Portland was to be with my mother and sister while my father had a serious operation, the first of too many that he had before his death four years later. So my memory of the frozen lake is also linked with that time, that worry and helplessness that was only the beginning of such feelings. Then, two years after that operation, another call came, the kind of call you dread and seem almost to understand before you pick up the phone. My mother was suddenly very sick and died within the year.

The frozen lake seemed to be the exact image of those years of cold trips to the hospital and bedside vigils. After they died my parents seemed to enter that frozen landscape of the past. So the lake began to assume greater weight while it moved farther into the past. There was also another experience that went along with this: when parents die, for a time at least, it seems they take your childhood—or some important part of it—with them just as they take the answers to all the questions you failed to ask, as well as the things you should have said but now can never say. I had spent the first eight years of my life beside that lake and now it seemed more remote than ever while it was also becoming a reservoir of grief and death.

Seeing the lake that time was one of those experiences that remains mysterious, hovering in the back of the mind, strange and troublesome. Clearly it does this because it resonates and rings out a deep but clouded response. Few experiences seem immediately symbolic but this seemed so to me: the past held there, frozen, waiting to thaw, but still inaccessible. I was thousands of feet above the scene and the plane was going along in its steady way, forcing the lake into the past. I felt that the lake would never thaw, of course, and that in some way our past is a kind of impenetrable winter, a winter so cold it goes far beyond the lowest temperatures ever recorded. But the scene nagged at me, demanding attention as it began to edge into the lines of poems not otherwise concerned with the Northwest or my own past. Now my parents were part of that frozen scene.

Then, some years later during a sabbatical in London, as if time and distance allowed for a partial thaw, the Northwest began to turn up fairly directly in poems. Over the next few years the poems became increasingly focused on Idaho and early memories.

And for the first time I was able to deal with my parents' lives and their deaths in my writing. Many of the new poems were based on what I call simple memory—that is, what I remembered easily or what I was told or overheard as a child. Such stories become our private legends and are part of memory, probably the easiest part. The results were poems about Idaho and the people there, and I felt I had an access, if not to the heart of the frozen lake, then at least to its edges. The people were farmers and loggers and wastrels, friends and enemies, the people of the Northwest who, for better or worse, made up the population that counted for me. The important thing was that it was local and particular. I feel that we understand a great deal only in terms of the local—as Patrick Kavanagh said, even *The Iliad* was just a local row after all.

As the poems written in England leaned toward and generated the Idaho poems, the Idaho poems in turn began to suggest another direction, a kind of night journey into the past. The frozen lake still needed to be reached and I was sent back to that view from the plane. The past and with it my sense of the Northwest swirled out of that frozen core, spiraling in the concentric circles caused by pebbles I dropped in it on some long ago summer day perhaps. Looking down from the plane that time, I remembered the smell of the lake, the odor of bark and water mixed with oil and gasoline from the summer people's fancy speedboats. Part of the effort of the new long poem I began to write was to try to reach the lake and thaw it back to life and thereby recapture the past whole. This is impossible of course but the past sometimes seems to demand such efforts.

Along the way in the poems about Idaho some discoveries were made. The first was that for me there was an almost Eden-like aura surrounding my early years beside the lake. Hence the wish, I suppose, in the long poem to thaw the whole area back to summer greenness. Next, it seemed that the poems were at least partly concerned with what has happened to this area—and the world—over the past fifty years or so. I had the feeling that something had been lost that can never be recovered. Here I am not suggesting an idyllic rural past—Idaho was scarcely that with those winters and the Depression, to say nothing of the narrowness and superstitiousness of many of the people. Rather I had a sense of something tough and honorable breaking up.

That sense of change has a good deal to do with politics in particular and in general. The early world I knew was poor but it wasn't mean, and it had about it the sense of everyone being in the same boat. If anything, the years since have gone the way of the summer people by the lake and everyone is now told to get his own boat. So part of what was locked in the frozen lake was, I suppose, that world which allowed for and encouraged compassion, and however garbled or dimly stated it was, there was a sense of generosity and a concern for values other than greed. Though there was a brief flowering in the Sixties, such feelings have suffered from the increasing privatization of life. Maybe the frozen lake also had something to do with the Cold War—the mean-spiritedness and the fear it has created, as well as its icy grip on the imagination.

Michael Harrington, rather optimistically in my view, says that compassion is a steady element in American society. To me the steady element now seems to be greed. But the Northwest has offered other examples. I remember the park built by the CCC's in McCall, and Wayne Morse's early and loud opposition to the war in Vietnam, as well as the first poetry reading against that war at Reed College. On good days I feel such voices are still here and that I'm not just hearing echoes from the past. Such things are important and make this a better place for a writer to live.

* * *

A few years ago I was returning to Portland from Southern Oregon but missed the express bus and the only available one was a local. Suddenly I felt as if I were driving through the past. The bus seemed to be seeking out all the little towns the freeway had erased. They were still there but pushed out of the way and ignored. And the people getting on the bus often seemed like my grandparents, my uncles and aunts, all suddenly resurrected. Because the bus stopped at every little town it could find, the ride seemed endless but remained fascinating because it was a small journey of discovery. I half-expected to come across the frozen lake and my parents as a young couple in the first years of their marriage. The pace of the ride allowed such fantasies which, I felt, the speed of the freeways would have blown away before they had a chance to form. I saw the freeways as a means of fleeing the past, a mode of travel like amnesia, in that typical American flight from history. The local bus sought out the past with the bus nosing along slowly and that ride became a variation on one of the central metaphors of my recent poems: the difficult night journey, the journey that demanded the invention of gravel roads and the resurrection of old cars like Reos and Model-B's or Hudsons. The freeway didn't suit my mode of transportation and thus didn't suit my sense of the Northwest which was decidedly off the beaten path, at most a wide place in the road like the small towns the local bus seemed to invent every few miles. But the towns were faded versions of the one I remembered, and while they were far from being ghost towns, they seemed to be sagging in that direction. The signs painted on the feed stores had almost flaked away. The whole bus ride seemed to parallel some of the things I was attempting in my poems—reversing the flight from the past and seeking it out, while also noting the decline in vitality and vividness that our age had brought about.

Part of my sense of the Northwest, then, is mixed up with this feeling of change and decline, and in a way it serves as both a private and a public metaphor. The local is crucial: we understand the world this way, just as we understand abstractions like honesty and love by how they actually manifest themselves in people we know. In McCall I heard stories of how the Roland boys fought the whole town of New Meadows. Or how my father spent three years tracking down, one by one, the three men who had ganged up on him at a dance. These were stories in the air that were in some ways comparable to the stories seen at the movies on Friday night or heard on the radio. I also recall a story my father told of some cattlemen from out of state who visited the valley one summer and thought it would be an ideal place to winter their herds. Apparently they wouldn't believe what the local people told them about the severity of the winters, and that part of the valley they used for their cattle was known for years afterward as The Boneyard, because every head of their large herd froze to death. Such stories, however grotesque some might be, were in the air and they gave that small town and valley a richness of meaning. The Boneyard story also dovetailed with my sense of the frozen lake. And there was that lake's monster as well, reports of which would come in periodically—especially early Sunday mornings after the bars closed. There were enough such reports to draw the attention of one of the national Sunday supplements and for one weekend the lake and its monster were famous. This was our genuine legend. But mixed with it were stories about Spencer Tracy and Robert

Young who spent one summer in McCall making the movie *Northwest Passage*. The Indian village built and burned in that movie was on the other side of the lake, and for years after that the area was known as Indian Village as if it had been a real one. There were even stories of people looking for rubber arrowheads and tomahawks.

I also remember my childhood visits "back home" after we moved to Portland after Pearl Harbor, and how my grandmother's house seemed to possess an aura and mystery unlike other houses. It was always exciting to go there. She was a strange, and I now realize, often malicious woman but she also had great charm and a very shrewd intelligence. She had homesteaded her own place in Eastern Oregon single-handed at the age of eighteen before marrying and moving to Idaho. Each of those visits awoke my early memories—times of swimming in the lake or skiing during winter or my fear of the bears in a nearby woods, bears invented by an uncle with a great talent for teasing. My memories differed from the reality of World War II which was made up of dusty, cramped apartments or nearly teeming housing projects—a world of strangers and potential violence somehow unlike the Roland boys' fights.

Given relatively healthy and calm early years in a family that cares about us, maybe we all have comparable memories of some Eden-like place that is lost when we become more aware of the world. But I can locate my place—McCall, Idaho. And for me it was now in a deep freeze that I had to try to thaw. But for me it is still at the core of my sense of this part of the world and serves as my touchstone.

* * *

I was flying from Iowa when I had my view—or vision—of the frozen lake. Before Iowa I had been in the army in Germany and had traveled a bit in Europe. Living in other places has also been a way of measuring the meaning of the Northwest. Without that experience, living here would be untested—no control would operate. I have spent some ten years living elsewhere: two years in England, over a year in Germany, and several years in Iowa, Minnesota, and Southern California. The times away from the stomping grounds have been good but there has always been a tinge of the unreal about them. In the Midwest I kept looking for mountains and listening for the Pacific. In the German Alps I caught hints of home but everything seemed miniaturized. In England the rain seemed almost familiar but the light and the air itself were different and here too a smaller scale prevailed, however pleasant and quaint that scale was. In California I found it hard to believe that palm trees weren't turned out in some hidden mill in the desert. Throughout these times of living elsewhere the touchstone remained the Northwest which bore the label, The Real World. And certainly no matter how cold it got elsewhere the frozen lake was nowhere near.

The local is crucial in ways difficult to define. Part of its importance is the familiar, the natural backdrop that seems like reality when we are elsewhere. It's not always a "good" reality of course, but it is the container for everything that counts—all joy and all grief, all ennui and all energy. Elsewhere there is a self-consciousness, the feeling of being a guest, and of finally not being responsible for what happens. Floods or storms are someone else's problem when you live elsewhere. It's like the experience of living in someone else's house where if something goes wrong you fix it but the problem isn't fraught with meaning the way it is in your own house where every breakdown seems an ominous comment on your life.

Mountains, rivers, lakes, and the Pacific were imprinted on me early and they seem the natural setting, the *right* landscape in which to carry on one's life. Or, since I'm no outdoorsman, the natural backdrop for the conduct of everyday life. Portland, too, seems a natural setting and, since it was my first and most persistent city, the likely size and shape for a city, just as Mt. Hood seems the right mountain. It also seems that on clear days you should be able to see a mountain. Even flat-topped St. Helens seems right. Now how such images and settings feed into one's work is mysterious. Clearly they penetrate deeper than consciousness, but I have no idea of precisely how this is done. They do have an influence though on the surrounding culture. Maybe they account for the humor of the Northwesterner, that irony and understatement which I like. Maybe it also accounts for the self-deprecatory nature of people here who act as if they knew we're all bound to lose in the fourth quarter no matter how far ahead we are at the half.

Such perceptions are sharpened by living elsewhere and, in fact, as was mentioned earlier, I had the experience of beginning to be able to use my past in the Northwest while living in England, nearly as far from this territory as I could get. But the distance and the feeling of a different kind of life around me seemed to trigger those poems. Certainly you never feel more American than when living in another country and my way of being an American, I saw, was to be a Northwesterner.

Distance and time gave perspective, and perspective of course is the key. Distance and time allow you to wait and see what will surface, and what surfaces is what counts. What began to emerge for me was the tip of the frozen lake with its classic seven-eighths still below the surface. Years have been spent getting at what was below that surface, inch by inch.

* * *

What has been said so far has been personal though I hope it has carried wider implications. Now it seems appropriate to consider some other literary issues, such as, is there in fact a Northwest tradition? One poet continues to preside over the Northwest: Theodore Roethke. Every poet in the area continues to owe a great deal to him. His presence in the Forties, Fifties, and early Sixties identified the Northwest as a region where poetry of national and international interest was produced. He also drew good poets to the area and though he clearly had his imitators, the range and diversity of his own work seemed to encourage similar diversity in others. The size of the Northwest, in fact, encourages diversity—writers often live far apart and may or may not see each other. Even in the cities no hothouse atmosphere exists. This fact of distance may also underscore for writers here the final reality of any writer's life—its isolation. Also because of the distances, some of the pettier aspects of the literary life seem diminished here—which isn't to say they don't exist.

For all artists in the Northwest there is another quality hard to nail down but decidedly present. This is the sense, perhaps in the weather itself, of Far-Eastern culture that is present and perhaps best shown in the work of such painters as Morris Graves and Mark Tobey. The presence of such painters also gave the area a legitimacy and artistic seriousness which enhances the atmosphere for writers. There was and is the feeling that something very good is going on here. That Roethke eventually lived in Graves' old house seemed to link the arts in the Northwest. So, though it is nearly impossible to delineate its features, there is the sense of a distinctive quality in work from the Pacific Northwest which persists with vitality and grace.

The nearness of the Pacific Ocean always serves as a source of perspective. Watching it or walking along its beaches seems to settle the spirit and what seems major in a city is reduced to its proper size. Or a walk in the woods or simply gazing at a mountain can also help when the world is too much with us. The key is that such places are readily accessible here and no major operation needs to be launched to experience them.

There are drawbacks too. I have eastern friends who assume I live on a ranch because I live in Oregon. Such misconceptions are amusing at times but not always. Yet here we have the advantage of provincials—we can know New York while New York doesn't know us. (And who even knows New York who only New York knows?) Still, if you are a Northwest writer, you know from the start that you're on a shunted sidetrack in a sense and that the culture of this country is skewed. You live with that. But that's old hat. It all reminds me of the Steinberg map of the U.S. that was on the cover of *The New Yorker* years ago. The foreground shows 9th and 10th Avenues with buildings that dwarf the rest of the map. Then comes a very wide Hudson River and beyond it is a rectangle, vaguely green and saying Jersey on the shore and scattered here and there are other place names—Chicago, Kansas City, Texas, Los Angeles, Utah, Las Vegas, Nebraska. There are no state lines, of course, and no Northwestern names. Steinberg was poking fun at Eastern provincialism but it's a provincialism that still exists and seems, if anything, to be renewed during these conservative years. But laughing with Steinberg seems the best response; that and getting on with our work by chipping away at our frozen lakes.

Tess Gallagher

Photo by Jim Heynen

TESS GALLAGHER grew up in Port Angeles, Washington. She began working as a journalist at the age of 16, and later studied with Theodore Roethke at the University of Washington. A graduate of the University of Iowa's M.F.A. Writing Program, she has taught at several universities, and is currently a member of the Graduate Writing Program Faculty at Syracuse University. Gallagher's poetry has brought her two National Endowment for the Arts grants, a Guggenheim Fellowship, and the Elliston Prize. She has traveled widely, including visits to Ireland and China. In addition to poetry, she has recently published a screenplay, and collections of fiction and of essays.

My Father's Love Letters

It's two days before Christmas and I have checked myself into the Dewitt Ranch Motel. "We don't ask questions here," says the manager, handing me the key to number 66. I let him think what he thinks.

The room is what I need, what I've been imagining for the past two days—a place with much passing and no record. I feel guilty about spending the money, but I've trusted my instincts about what it will take to get this writing done. For the past week I've been absorbed with student manuscripts and term papers. At the finish, I discover I have all but vanished. Coming to the motel is a way to trick myself out of anonymity, to urge my identity to rise like cream to the top again.

I had known from the first moments of being asked to write about my influences as a writer that I would want to get back to the child in me. For to talk of influences for a writer is essentially to trace the development of a psychic and spiritual history, to go back to where it keeps starting as you think about it, as an invention of who you are becoming. The history which has left its deepest imprint on me has been an oral and actual history and so involves my willingness at a very personal level. It involves people no one will ever know again. People like the motel room I write this in, full of passing and no record. The "no record" part is where I come in. I must try to interrupt their silence. Articulate it and so resurrect them so that homage can be paid.

To speak of influences, then, is not to say "Here, try this," only "This happened and this is what I think of it at this moment of writing."

* * *

I want to begin with rain. A closeness, a need for rain. It is the climate of my psyche and I would not fully have known this if I had not spent a year in Arizona, where it rained only three glorious times during my entire stay there. I begin with rain also because it is a way of introducing my birthplace on the Olympic Peninsula in Washington State, the town of Port Angeles. The rain forest is a few miles west. The rain is more violent and insistent there. Port Angeles lies along the Strait of Juan de Fuca and behind the town are the Olympic Mountains. The Japanese current brings in warm air, striking the mountains, which are snow-covered into June.

It is a faithful rain. You feel it has some allegiance to the trees and the people, to the little harbor with its long arm of land which makes a band of calm for the fishing boats and for the rafts of logs soon to be herded to the mills. Inside or outside the wood-frame houses, the rain pervades the temperament of the people. It brings an ongoing thoughtfulness to their faces, a meditativeness that causes them to fall silent for long periods, to stand at their windows looking out at nothing in particular. The people don't mind getting wet. Galoshes, umbrellas—there isn't a market for them here. The people walk in the rain as within some spirit they wish not to offend with resistance. Most of them have not been to Arizona. They know the rain is a reason for not living where they live, but they live there anyway. They work hard in the logging camps, in the pulp mills and lumberyards. Everything has a wetness over it, glistening quietly as though it were still in the womb, waiting to be born.

Growing up there, I thought the moss-light that lived with us lived everywhere. It was a sleepy predawn light that muted the landscape and made the trees come close. I always went outside with my eyes wide, no need to shield them from sun bursts or the steady assault of skies I was to know later in El Paso or Tucson. The colors of green and gray are what bind me to the will to write poems.

Along with rain and a subdued quality of light, I have needed the nearness of water. I said once in an interview that if Napoleon had stolen his battle plans from the dreams of his sleeping men, then maybe I had stolen my poems from the gray presence of water.

The house I grew up in overlooks the eighteen-mile stretch of water between Canada and America at its far northwest reach. The freighters, tankers, tugs, and small fishing boats pass daily; and even at night a water star, the light on a mast, might mark a vessel's passage through the strait. My father was a longshoreman for many of these years and he knew the names of the ships and what they were carrying and where they came from: the *Kenyo Maru* (Japanese), the *Eastern Grace* (Liberian), the *Bright Hope* (Taiwanese), the *Brilliant Star* (Panamanian), the *Shoshei Maru* (Japanese)—pulp for paper, logs for plywood, lumber for California.

He explained that *Maru* was a word that meant that the ship would make its return home. I have been like these ships, always pointed on a course of return to this town and its waters.

* * *

On Saturdays my father would drive my mother and my three brothers and me into town to shop and then to wait for him while he drank in what we called the "beer joints." We would sit for hours in the car, watching the townspeople pass. I noticed what they carried, how they walked, their gestures as they looked into the store windows. In other cars were women and families waiting as we were, for men in taverns. In the life of a child, these periods of stillness in parked cars were small eternities. The only release or amusement was to see things, and to wonder about them. Since the making of images is for me perhaps ninety percent seeing and ten percent word power, this car-seeing and the stillness it enforced contributed to a patience and a curiosity that heightened my ability to see. The things to be seen from a parked car were not spectacular, but they were what we had—and they promoted a fascination with the ordinary. My mother was an expert at this: "See that little girl with the pigtails. I bet she's never had her hair cut. Look there, her father's taking her in there where men get their hair cut." And sure enough, the little girl would emerge twenty minutes later, eyes red from crying, one hand in her father's and the other clutching a small paper sack. "The pigtails are in there."

Every hour or so my mother would send me on a round of the taverns to try for a sighting of my father. I would peck on the windows and the barmaid would shake her head *no* or motion down the dim aisle of faces to where my father would be sitting on his stool, forgetting, forgetting us all for a while.

My father's drinking, and the quarrels he had with my mother because of it, terrorized my childhood. There is no other way to put it. And if coping with terror and anxiety are necessary to the psychic stamina of a poet, I had them in steady doses—just as inevitably as I had the rain. I learned that the world was not just, that any balance was temporary, that unreasonableness could descend at any minute, thrashing aside everything and everyone in its path.

Emotional and physical vulnerability was a constant. Yet the heart began to take shelter, to build understandings out of words.

It seems that a poet is one who must be strong enough to live in the unprotected openness, yet not so strong that the heart enters what the Russian poet Akhmatova calls "the icy calm of unloving." Passion and forgiveness, emotional fortitude—these were the lessons of the heart I had no choice but to learn in my childhood. I wonder now what kept me from the calm of not loving. Perhaps it was the unspoken knowledge that love, my parents' love, through all was constant, though its blows could rake the quick of my being.

I was sixteen when I had my last lesson from the belt and my father's arm. I stood still in the yard, in full view of the neighbors. I looked steadily ahead, without tears or cries, as a tree must look while the saw bites in, then deepens to the core. I felt my spirit reach its full defiance. I stood somehow in the power of my womanhood that day and knew I had passed beyond humiliation. I felt my father's arm begin to know I had outleaped the pain. It came down harder. If pain could not find me, what then would enforce control and fear?

I say I entered my womanhood because I connect womanhood with a strong, enduring aspect of my being. I am aware, looking back, that women even more than children often serve a long apprenticeship to physically inflicted threat and pain. Perhaps because of this they learn more readily what the slave, the hostage, the prisoner, also know—the ultimate freedom of the spirit. They learn how unreasonable treatment and physical pain may be turned aside by an act of the will. This freedom of spirit is what has enabled poets down through the ages to record the courage and hopes of entire peoples even in times of oppression. That women have not had a larger share in the history of such poetry has always seemed a mystery to me, considering the wealth of spiritual power that suffering often brings when it does not kill or maim the spirit. I can only assume that words have been slow in coming to women because their days have, until recently, been given over so wholly to acts, to doing and caring for.

I did not feel sorry for myself during these periods of abuse and I did not stop loving. It was our hurt not to have another way to settle these things. For my father and I had no language between us in those numb years of my changing. All through my attempts in the poems, I have needed to forge a language that would give these dead and living lives a way to speak. There was often the feeling that the language might come too late, might even do damage, might not be equal to the love. All these fears. Finally no choice.

The images of these two primal figures, mother and father, condense now into a vision of my father's work-thickened hands, and my mother's back, turned in hopeless anger at the stove where she fixed eggs for my father in silence. My father gets up from the table, shows me the open palms of his hands. "Threasie," he says, "get an education. Don't get hands like these."

Out of this moment and others like it I think I began to make a formula which translates roughly: words = more than physical power = freedom from enslavement to job-life = power to direct and make meaning in your own life.

There were few examples of my parents' having used words to transcend the daily. The only example was perhaps my father's love letters. They were kept in a cedar chest at the foot of my bed. One day I came across them, under a heap of hand-embroidered pillowcases. There were other treasures there, like the deer horn used to call the hounds when my father had hunted as a young man. The letters were written on lined tablet paper with a yellow cast to it. Written with a pencil in a consistently erratic hand, signed "Les" for Leslie and punctuated with a brigade of *XXXXX*'s. I would stare at these *X*'s, as though they contained some impenetrable clue as to why this man and woman had come together. The letters were mainly informational – he had worked here, was going there, had seen so-and-so, would be coming back to Missouri at such-and-such a time. But also there was humor, harmless jokes some workman had told him, and little teasings that only my mother could have interpreted.

My mother's side of the correspondence was missing, probably because my father had thrown her letters away or lost them during the Depression years when he crossed the country, riding the rails, working in the cotton fields, the oil fields, and the coal mines. My mother's lost letters are as important to remember as those I found from my father. They were the now invisible lifeline that answered and provoked my father's heart-scrawl across the miles and days of their long courtship. I might easily have called this essay "My Mother's Love Letters," for they would have represented the most articulate half of the correspondence, had they been saved. That they are now irrevocably lost, except to the imagination, moves them into the realm of speculation. The very fact that my mother had saved my father's love letters became a sign to me as a child that love *had* existed between my parents, no matter what acts and denials might come after.

As with my parents, invisible love has been an undercurrent in my poems, in the tone of them, perhaps. They have, when I can manage it, what Marianne Moore called iodine and what I call turpentine. A rawness of impulse, a sharpness, a tension, that complicates the emotion, that withholds even as it gives. This is a proclivity of being, the signature of a nature that had learned perhaps wrongheadedly that love too openly seen becomes somehow inauthentic, unrealized.

My father's love letters were then the only surviving record of my parents' courtship and, indeed, the only record that they ever loved each other, for they never showed affection for one another in front of us. On a fishing trip years after I'd left home, my father was to remark that they had written to each other for over ten years before they married in 1941.

My father's sleep was like the rain. It permeated the household. When he was home he seemed always to be sleeping. We saw him come home and we saw him leave. We saw him during the evening meal. The talk then was of the ILWU longshoremen's union and of the men he worked with. He worked hard. It could be said that he never missed a day's work. It was a fact I used in his defense when I thought my mother was too hard on him after a drinking bout.

Stanley Kunitz has seen the archetypal search for the father as a frequent driving force for some poets, his own father having committed suicide before his birth. It occurs to me that in my own case, the father was among the living dead, and this made my situation all the more urgent. It was as if I had set myself the task of waking him before it was too late. I seemed to need to tell him who he was and that what was happening to him mattered and was witnessed by at least one other. This is why he has been so much at the center of my best efforts in the poems.

The first poem I wrote that reached him was called "Black Money," this image taken from the way shoveling sulfur at the pulp mills had turned his money black. He had come to visit me in the Seattle apartment where I lived as a student and I remember telling him I'd written this poem for his birthday. I had typed it and sealed it into an envelope like a secret message. He seemed embarrassed, as if about to be left out of something. Then he tore the envelope open and unfolded the poem. He handed it back to me. "You read it to me," he said. I read the poem to him and as I read I could feel the need in his listening. I had finally reached him. "Now that's something," he said when I'd finished. "I'm going to show that to the boys down on the dock."

As the oldest child, I seemed to serve my parents' lives in an ambassadorial capacity. But I was an ambassador without a country, for the household was perpetually on the verge of dissolving. I cannot say how many times I watched my father go down the walk to the picket fence, leaving us forever, pausing long enough at the gate to look back at us huddled on the porch. "Who's coming with me?" he would ask. No one moved. Again and again we abandoned each other.

Maybe this was the making of my refugee mentality. And perhaps when you are an emotional refugee you learn to be industrious toward the prospect of love and shelter. You know both are fragile and that stability must lie with you or it is nowhere. You make a home of yourself. Words for me and later poems were the tools of that home-making.

Even when you think you are only a child and have nothing, there are things you have, and as Sartre has already told us, one of these things is words. When I say I had words and that these could affect what happened to me and those I loved, I felt less powerless, as though these might win through, might at least mediate in a life ruled as much by chance as by intention.

These ambassadorial skills I was learning as a child were an odd kind of training for the writing of poems, perhaps, but they were just that. For in the writing of the poem you must represent both sides of the question. If not in fact, then in understanding. You must bring them into dialogue with one another fairly, without the bias of causes or indignation or needing too much to be right. It requires a widening of perspective, away from oversimplification—the strict good or bad, wrong or rightness of a situation. The sensibility I've been attempting to write out of wants to represent the spectrum of awareness. In this way the life is accounted for in its fullness, when I am able.

I have spoken of words as a stay against unreasonableness, and they are often this—though more to one's solitude than to the actual life. My father came to his own words late, but in time. I was to discover that at seventy he could entertain my poet friends and would be spoken of afterward as someone exceptional in their experience. He told stories, was witty, liked to laugh. But in those early days, my father was not a man you could talk with. He would drive me to my piano lessons, the family's one luxury, without speaking. He smoked cigarettes, one after the other. He was thinking and driving. If he had had anything to drink during these times it was best to give him a wide berth. I was often afraid of him, of the violence in him, though like the rain, tenderness was there, unspoken and with a fiber that strangely informed even the unreasonable. If to be a poet is to balance contraries, to see how seemingly opposite qualities partake of, in fact penetrate, each other, I learned this from my combative parents.

This long childhood period of living without surety contributed in another way to my urge to write poetry. If I had to give one word which serves my poetry more than any other, it might be "uncertainty." Uncertainty which leads to exploration, to the articulation of fears, to the loss of the kind of confidence that provides answers too quickly, too superficially. It is the poet's uncertainty which leaves her continually in an openness to the possibilities of being and saying. The true materials of poetry are essentially invisible—a capacity for the constant emptying of the house of the word, turning it out homeless and humbled to search its way toward meaning again. Maybe "poem" for me is the act of a prolonged beginning, one without resolution except perhaps musically, rhythmically—the word "again" engraved on the fiery hammer.

After my youngest brother's death when I was twenty, I began to recognize the ability of poetry to extend the lives of those not present except in memory. My brother's death was the official beginning of my mortality. It filled my life, all our lives, with the sense of an unspoken bond, a pain which traveled with us in memory. It was as though memory were a kind of flickering shadow left behind by those who died. This caused me to connect memory firmly to the life of the spirit and finally to write poems which formalized the sharing of that memory.

I have been writing about my progress toward a life in words and poems, but my first love was actually paint. As a child I took great pleasure in the smell of linseed, the oil of it on my fingers, the tubes of oil paint with their bands of approximate color near the caps, the long-handled brushes. I had heard somewhere that artists taught themselves by copying other painters. But the only paintings we had in the house were those in some Bible books a salesman had sold my mother. I began to copy these with oil colors onto some rough paper I'd found in a boxcar near the paper mill below our house. I remember especially my painting of Jacob sleeping at the foot of a heavenly stairway, with several angels descending. They each had a pair of huge wings and I wondered at the time why they didn't just fly down, instead of using the stairs. The faces of these angels occupied a great deal of my efforts. And I think it is some help to being a poet to paint the faces of angels when you are ten.

I finished the Jacob painting and sent it to my grandfather in Missouri. He was a farmer and owned a thousand-acre farm of scrub oak, farmland, and riverbed in the Ozarks. My mother had been raised there. Often when she had a faraway look about her, I imagined she was visiting there in her thoughts.

Children sometimes adopt a second father or mother when they are cut off from the natural parent. Porter Morris, my uncle, was the father I could speak with. He lived with my grandparents on the farm in Windyville, Missouri, where I spent many of my childhood summers. He never married, but stayed with the farm even after my grandparents had died. He'd been a mule trainer during the Second World War, the only time he had ever left home. He loved horses and raised and gentled one for me, which he named Angel Foot because she was black except for one white foot.

I continued to visit my grandfather and my uncle during the five years of my first marriage. My husband was a jet pilot in the Marine Corps. We were stationed in the South, so I would go to cook for my uncle during the haying and I would also help stack the hay in the barn. My uncle and I took salt to the cattle. We sowed a field with barley and went to market in Springfield with a truckload of pigs. There were visits with neighbors, Cleydeth and Joe Stefter or Jule Elliot, when we sat for hours telling stories and gossiping. Many images from my uncle's stories and from these visits to the farm got into the long poem "Songs of the Runaway Bride" in my first book.

My uncle lived alone at the farm after my grandfather's death, but soon he met a woman who lived with her elderly parents. He began to remodel an old house on the farm. There was talk of marriage. One day my mother called to say there had been a fire at the farm. The house had burned to the ground and my uncle could not be found. She returned to the farm, what remained of her childhood home. After the ashes had cooled, she searched with the sheriff and found my uncle's skeleton where it had burned into the mattress springs of the bed.

My mother would not accept the coroner's verdict that the fire had been caused by an electrical short-circuit, or a fire in the chimney. It was summer and no fire would have been laid. She combed the ashes looking for the shotgun my uncle always kept near his bed and the other gun, a rifle, he hunted with. They were not to be found. My mother believed her brother had been murdered and she set about proving it. She offered a reward and soon after, a young boy walking along the roadside picked my uncle's billfold out of the ditch, his name stamped in gold on the flap.

Three men were eventually brought to trial. I journeyed to Bolivar, Missouri, to meet my parents for the trial. We watched as the accused killer was released and the other two men, who had confessed to being his accomplices, were sentenced to five years in the penitentiary for manslaughter. Parole would be possible for them in two to three years. The motive had been money, although one of the men had held a grudge against my uncle for having been ordered to move out of a house he'd been renting from my uncle some three years before. They had taken forty dollars from my uncle, then shot him when he could not give them more. My parents and I came away from the trial stunned with disbelief and anger.

I tried to write it out, to investigate the nature of vengeance, to disarm myself of the anger I carried. I wrote two poems about this event, "Two Stories" and "The Absence." Images from my uncle's death also appeared in "Stepping Outside," the title poem of my first, limited-edition collection. I began to see poems as a way of settling scores with the self. I felt I had reached the only possible justice in the writing out of my anger and the honoring of the life that had been taken so brutally. The *In Cold Blood* aspect of my uncle's murder has caused violence to haunt my vision of what it is to live in America. Sometimes, with my eyes wide open, I still see the wall behind my grandfather's empty bed, and on it, the fiery angels and Jacob burning.

I felt if my uncle, the proverbial honest man, could be murdered in the middle of the night, then anything was possible. The intermittent hardships of my childhood were nothing compared to this. I saw how easily I could go into a state of fear and anger which would mar the energy of my life and consequently my poems for good. I think I began, in a steady way, to move toward accepting my own death, so that whenever it would come before me as a thought, I would release myself toward it. In the poems I've written that please me most, I seem able to see the experience with dead-living eyes, with a dead-living heart.

My own sense of time in poems approximates what I experience in my life—that important time junctures of past and present events via memory and actual presences are always inviting new meanings, revisions of old meanings, and speculation about things still in the future. These time shifts are a special province of poems because they can happen there more quickly, economically, and convincingly that in any other art form, including film. Film is still struggling to develop a language of interiority using the corporeal image, while even words like *drum* and *grief* in poems can borrow inflection from the overlap of words in context, can form whole new entities, as in a line from Louise Bogan's poem "Summer Wish": "The drum pitched deep as grief."

Since my intention here has been to emphasize experiential influences rather than literary ones, I must speak of the Vietnam War, for it was the war that finally caused me to take up my life as a poet. For the first time since I had left home for college, I was thrown back on my own resources. My husband and I had met when I was eighteen and married when I was twenty-one. I was twenty-six when he left to fly missions in Vietnam. I'd had very little life on my own. It became a time to test my strengths. I began working as a ward clerk in a hospital, on the medical floor. I did this for about five months, while the news of the war arrived daily in my mailbox. I was approaching what a friend of that time called an "eclipse." He urged me to leave the country. It was the best decision I could have made, as I look back now.

My time in Ireland and Europe during the Vietnam War put me firmly in possession of my own life. But in doing this, it made my life in that former time seem fraudulent. The returning veterans, my husband among them, had the hardship of realizing that many Americans felt the war to be wrong. This pervasive judgment was a burden to us both and one that eventually contributed to the dissolution of our marriage.

I began to experience a kind of psychic suffocation which expressed itself in poems that I copied fully composed from my dreams. For a while, this disassociation of dream material from my life caused the messages to go unheeded. But gradually my movement out of the marriage began to enact the images of dissolution in the poems. It was a parting that gave me unresolvable grief, yet at the same time allowed my life its first true joys as I began a full commitment to my writing. I think partings have often informed my poems with a backward longing, and it was especially so with this one.

I returned to Seattle in 1969 and began to study poetry with David Wagoner at the University of Washington. My family did not understand what I was doing. Why should I divorce and then go back to college to learn to write poetry? It was beyond them. What was going to become of me now? Who would take care of me?

* * *

Trees have always been an important support to the solitude I connect with the writing of poetry. I suspect my affection and need of them began in those days in my childhood when I was logging with my parents. There was a coolness in the forest, a feeling of light filtering down from the arrow-shaped tops of the evergreens. The smell of pitch comes back. The chain-saw snarl and a spray of wood chips. Sawdust in the cuffs of my jeans. My brothers and I are again the woodcutter's children. We play under the trees, but even our play is a likeness to work. We construct shelters of rotten logs, thatch them with fireweed, and then invite our parents into the shelters to eat their lunches. We eat Spam sandwiches and smoked fish, with a Mountain Bar for dessert. After a time, my parents give me a little hatchet and a marking stick so I can work with them, notching the logs to be cut up into pulpwood to be made into paper. My brothers and I strip cones from the fallen trees, milking the hard pellets with our bare hands into gunnysacks, which are sold to the Forestry Department for ten dollars a bag. There is a living to be made and all of us are expected to do our share.

This word *share* has become a sadly lost word in American life. Children seem not to be taught sharing as we were. It seems a part of my attitude toward being a poet—that my writing serve not only my own life but the lives of others, the community at large.

When I think of it now, it is not far from the building of those makeshift shelters to the making of poems. You take what you find, what comes naturally to the hand and mind. There was the sense with these shelters that they wouldn't last, but that they were exactly what could be done at the time. There were great gaps between the logs because we couldn't notch them into each other, but this allowed us to see the greater forest between them. It was a house that remembered its forest. And for me, the best poems, no matter how much order they make, have an undercurrent of forest, of the larger unknown.

To spend one's earliest days in a forest with a minimum of supervision gave a lot of time for exploring. I also had some practice in being lost. Both exploring and being lost are, it seems now, the best kind of training for a poet. When I think of those times I was lost, it comes back with a strange exhilaration, as though I had died, yet had the possibility of coming back to life. The act of writing a poem is like that. It is that sense of aloneness which is trying to locate the world again, but not too soon, not until the voice has made its cry, "Here, here, over here," and the answering voices have called back, "Where are you?"

My mother and father started logging together in 1941, the year my mother traveled from Missouri by bus to marry my father. As far as she knows, she was the only woman who worked in the woods, doing the same work the men did. She was mainly the choker-setter and haul-back. She hauled the heavy steel cable, used to yard the logs into the landing, out over the underbrush to be hooked around the fallen trees. My mother's job was a dangerous one because the trees, like any dying thing, would often thrash up unexpectedly or release underbrush which could take out an eye or lodge in one's side. She also lifted and stacked the pulpwood onto the truck and helped in the trimming of the branches. She did this work for seven years.

There is a photograph of my mother sitting atop two gigantic logs in her puffed-sleeved blouse and black work pants. It has always inspired me with a pride in my sex. I think I grew up with the idea that whatever the rest of the world said about women, the woman my mother was stood equal to any man and maybe one better. Her labor was not an effort to prove anything to anyone. It was what had to be done for the living. I did not think of her as unusual until I was about fourteen. I realized then that she was a wonderful mechanic. She could fix machines, would take them apart and reassemble them. None of the mothers of my friends had such faith in their own abilities. She was curious and she taught herself. She liked to tinker, to shift a situation or an object around. She had an eye for possibilities and a faculty for intuitive decision-making that afterward looked like knowledge. I feel I've transferred to the writing of poems many of my mother's explorative methods, even a similar audacity toward my materials.

* * *

"What happened to those letters?" I ask my mother over the telephone. I don't tell her I'm at the Dewitt Ranch Motel writing this essay. I don't tell her I'm trying to understand why I keep remembering my father's love letters as having an importance to my own writing.

"Well, a lot of them were sent to the draft board," she says. "Your dad and I were married November of forty-one. Pearl Harbor hit December seventh, so they were going to draft your father. A lot of men was just jumping up to get married to avoid the draft. We had to prove we'd been courting. The only way was to send the letters, so they could see for themselves."

"But what happened to the letters?"

"There was only about three of them left. You kids got into them, so I burnt them."

"You burnt them? Why? Why'd you do that?"

"They wasn't nothing in them."

"But you kept them," I say. "You saved them."

"I don't know why I did," she says. "They didn't amount to anything."

I hang up. I sit on one of the two beds and stare out at an identical arm of the motel which parallels the unit I'm in. I think of my father's love letters being perused by the members of the draft board. They become convinced that the courtship is authentic. They decide not to draft him into the war. As a result of his having written love letters, he does not go to his death, and my birth takes place. It is an intricate chain of events, about which I had no idea at the start of this essay.

I think of my father's love letters burning, of how they might never have come into their true importance had I not returned to them here in my own writing. I sit in the motel room, a place of much passage and no record, and feel I have made an important assault on the Great Nothing, though the letters are gone, though they did not truly exist until this writing, even for my parents, who wrote and received them.

My father's love letters are the sign of a long courtship and I pay homage to that, the idea of writing as proof of the courtship – the same blind, persistent hopefulness that carries me again and again into poems.

Paul Pintarich

Photo by Dana Olsen

PAUL PINTARICH was born and raised in Portland. A graduate of Portland State University, he has worked as Columbia River tugboat crewman, Navy hospital corpsman, and since 1965 as newspaperman at *The Oregonian*. He's covered a variety of beats, including police, urban affairs, business, labor, transportation and planning. Since 1982 he has concentrated on books and publishing. He is currently the Literary Arts Editor for *The Oregonian's* Northwest magazine.

Our Linoleum Age

Between the Great Depression and the acknowledged beginnings of the "atomic age"—somewhere in the mid-1950s—there was a halcyon period we might label "our linoleum age," an age that formed a generation of storytellers.

This was a time when the mass of "baby boomers" was still in diapers or merely a twinkle in the old man's eyes, when "the bomb" would be brought forth to end one war but never to start another; when remote Western cities, for the most part, contained themselves, and just beyond their limits grazing cows could never imagine the polluting press of suburbia.

Once, when I was very young, my father held up a glass of tap water and said proudly, "Look at that! Bull Run water, the best in the world!"

There were no chemicals in the water then, not one, and it was sweet and cold.

That it also had no minerals—and many of us had bad teeth—made no difference. This was the Pacific Northwest, and the water was a symbol of how fresh and hopeful everything still was. Salmon and smelt still ran up the rivers in great numbers, and I can remember logging trucks fully loaded with only one bucked section of massive trees.

I remember those things. And, as I grow older with what seems to be terrible swiftness, I remember many other things from the past as well; the stuff of a writer's mind, trivia once laughed over but now suddenly valuable in explaining our lives.

When I was three the Japanese attacked Pearl Harbor. I can remember only a few moments of that day, but it was sunny and my father jumped from the woodshed roof, crashed through the back screen door and, commandeering the radio, wouldn't let my mother or me say anything until President Roosevelt had finished droning his promise of revenge.

What I have come to remember more, however, is that my father, who built the tiny three-room house with the help of a drunk and a mule, moved into the war years across a floor of linoleum. In doing so he passed a hand-wringer washing machine, a woodstove cooling after breakfast pancakes and an icebox, an oaken one shiny with strong brass fittings.

We lived then on an early nibble into the pasture of a once grand dairy farm that, because of economic exigencies after the death of its Swiss founder, was being sold in bits and pieces by his widow.

She was a tough, plodding woman who roamed her neighborhood in men's hightop shoes, her head wrapped like a Navajo against the painful herpes blisters that tormented her forehead. I was a mere lad when I watched her axe a chicken for her dinner, and, since it was my first decapitation, I was amused rather than shocked by its running around in blind-mute frenzy.

But that chicken, and the ones my grandmother raised on a small farm a "little farther out," had a flavor some feel is gone forever. Like milk in bottles with cream on top, or warm milk right out of the cow. There were vegetables delivered in galvenized buckets by noisy Italians, and a bread man from Multnomah who brought unsliced loaves and glazed donuts conceived in some small boy's imagination.

Though we lived only several short miles from downtown Portland, there was a working barn across the street, fat trout in Tryon Creek and deep woods that crawled over and around the small West Hills, and which covered Mount Sylvania, a weathered shield volcano that took the brunt of Pacific storms on its southwest flank.

We used to climb that mountain in the sun and in the wind and rain, seeking out squirrels, raccoons, pheasants and the occasional deer, though, despite our heroic intent, we would never have killed them with our single-shot twenty twos.

You could see for miles up there among the snags and rocks and young firs. You could see Oregon City and the Willamette River and, to the west, the Coast Range; at night you wouldn't see any lights, hardly, where now there is only homes and sprawl and freeway noise.

Many years later I crawled up there for some peace of mind and confronted a security guard who, apparently, was concerned for a pump chugging noisily there, at a place where we used to camp. He asked what I thought I was doing, and I told him I knew what I was doing, revisiting my childhood, a time when he hadn't been born.

I remembered, wrote a poem and got to thinking. There was no asphalt on the schoolyard, wicker-seated streetcars clanged and banged, all the first-run movie houses were downtown and nights were safe for unlocked doors.

My grandfather, a tailor from Yugoslavia who spoke three languages but not English very well, would wear an immaculate three-piece suit and leather, "snake-hunter" gaiters when we carried our telescoping fishing rods aboard the "interurban" for a ride to the ponds behind Oaks Park.

Why did I remember that and keep it somewhere? That the stores were closed on Saturday, when many people worked half-days, and on Sundays we mustered at grandma's for huge, million-caloried meals? How everyone sat in the kitchen in the evenings, aunts, uncles, mothers, fathers, kids, speaking a warm patois of English and Serbo-Croatian, but mostly "Croat" when the adults began discussing how things were when they left "the old country."

My Slavic grandmother, trained as a cook in Austria, kept a woodstove until the late 1950s; my Icelandic grandmother, mother of my mother, kept a garden, cows, later goats, and lived with my stepgrandfather, a former poacher and blacksmith who joined and was active in the German-American Bund before World War II.

This stepgrandfather was kind in a rough-hewn way. During World War II, when my grandparents had taken a farm from a deposed Japanese farmer, I spent summers sleeping in an upstairs room papered with Japanese characters. I was only five or so, but I blithely learned about haying, Hitler and horseshoeing, and became familiar as well with a cantankerous ex-Army mule whose personality matched that of the old man.

"Them sonsofbitches!" he liked to say, rocking in his bibby overalls, his pipe reeking of Prince Albert, telling me about Nostradamus, star signs and how "Hitler gave them people bathtubs!"

My parents were divorced about this time, and I remember a lot of linoleum and oilcloth table coverings in the homes where I moved about. I remember how hard linoleum was lying before a briquet-fed "Cheerio" stove or oil heater, and how cold when bare feet took the shock of a winter morning.

And outhouses. Try one of those when your foggy mind must decide, at three on a snowy morning, whether to dash for it or simply let your bladder burst in an explosion of warm pain.

You try to remember what you know. And since I was born here, in Portland, I try to remember all I can. Creeping through the woods, for example, the night-lighted shipyards of World War II; the Vanport Flood—Hey! And remember . . .?

You remember these things when you grow older, and you know what is meant when old guys are accused of remembering too much. So you want to write them down before you get so old they seem trite in your mind and your energy is gone.

You want to write it all down because the world has changed so fast that younger people, even the baby boomers, have overextended their heritage and snapped any links with tradition.

In the old days there were storytellers. My Uncle Marko told once how he left the old country and crossed France by hiding in the trenches left from World War I. He was caught by French police at Verdun, and it took some time to question him because no one spoke Serbo-Croatian.

Everybody in the family, on both sides, told stories. Winter Sundays we would gather at grandma's and eat too much and tell stories. Summer Sundays, we would gather at grandma's, eat too much and sit outside telling stories, spitting seeds if it was warm and we had watermelon.

And when we were alone we could listen to the radio, which you could do and do something else at the same time. On Sunday evenings we had to listen to the radio because of Jack Benny, but, and more important, because Uncle Stanko had a radio program, "Old Dusty," which, to be honest, was as dry as dust.

But God! The radio. What a wonderful instrument. You could build model airplanes and read a book and still listen to the radio. You could listen to the radio and scenes would swirl and form in your mind; today, hearing old radio programs, I imagine the same all over again. You didn't have to stare at the damn thing.

All of this, feeling it, being able to remember it all, is perhaps what makes a writer. Who knows?

But there's one thing. One sure thing. Growing up on the floors of that linoleum age, we were a mere handful, children of parents reluctant to have children in hard times. It made us unique in a way, because between our parents' generation and that of the baby boomers, we assumed the role of translators, a role we maintain today.

When all about us the world is fraught with disarray, we can answer some with, "Well, it's been that way before." We can also say that it will be that way again. And to learn, perhaps to survive, we try to tell them the stories of our linoleum age.

To do this we write—and well, I hope—because we are a generation of storytellers.

Vi Gale

Photo by Jerome Hart

VI GALE was born in Norest, Dala-Jarna, Sweden, and is a naturalized U.S. citizen. She studied creative writing and poetry at Portland State University and at Lewis and Clark College. In a career that has spanned over 30 years, Gale has published six collections of poetry, including her most recent book *Odd Flowers & Short-Eared Owls*. Her work has appeared in a wide variety of prestigious literary magazines. She has taught numerous workshops, and for the last 12 years has been editor and publisher at Prescott Street Press.

The Negotiating Eye: Is There a Northwest Outlook?

A good question. Certainly some of us who have been in the writing field for a long time have heard how colleagues from other places look at *us*:

"There's a writer under every rock." "Such cowboys. Justin boots and Stetson hats. They roar around in pickup trucks and drink everything out of *mugs*." "The men are macho chauvinists and the women, even the feminists, are frustrated botanists." "Their poets write novels and play baseball." "Their novelists milk cows and write bestsellers that get made into movies." "They translate Sappho with fierce fidelity." "The poets exile themselves to China, Japan, and Greece." "Trekkies, sci-fies and scholars—when they aren't humanists practicing self-expression." "They say it isn't anthropomorphic, it's Native American."

Easy stereotypes, of course. But editors on the other side of the Mississippi sometimes imply that we don't know alba from zeugma from Elizabethan rant from seven types of ambiguity and that we are all drunk on landscape. Sometimes we mildly mutter back:

From Oregon on a Slightly Less Green Leaf

"Sorry. We don't use nature poetry. Ours is an urban society."
— *Eastern editor*

"May we see some more of you ecology poems?"
— *Same editor, fifteen years later*

I'm still here, barefoot and lank-haired,
at the rocky edge of the same ocean
studded with arches, caverns and stacks.

My song is about what it was. Thorny.
Low-key as wild blackberry vines circling
old logging spars on the burns.

Inland, the same native rockroses hug
their volcanic ground under high desert sky.
At night you can still breathe in the stars.

But you had a point. We lobby and legislate,
preserve dunes, purify rivers, save rain
forests, religiously lug back the beer bottles.

At that, pollution now hangs over snowcaps.
Dams and ladders threaten our salmon. Freeways
kill neighborhoods. Towns choke on themselves.

(Vi Gale, *Odd Flowers & Short-Eared Owls*)

If we get too paranoid about criticism we go wind surfing, skiing or huckleberry picking. This does not mean that we aren't serious or dedicated to our work. Or that we are being as independent as our maverick politicians. Often it is a case of give the horse its head and it will take you home.

We even kid each other. One year a student came home from the Haystack Conference and told me that the late Richard F. Hugo had said I couldn't use the word "salal" because it belonged to Hugo. Dick, wherever you are, I can hear you laughing. That student believed you, and she has probably distrusted certain specifics and particulars ever since.

The good writers of the Northwest are careful about merely dropping place names or zeroing in on landmarks—especially when depicting the old or abandoned which are easily made sentimental. We do have levels of meaning in what we write.

In an early poem, written about 1955, I was trying to sort out some of these things. I wrote about the Elk Fountain that stands in the middle of a downtown Portland street, noting that "it stares unblinkingly Northwest." The poem speaks of "an anachronistic beast . . . linked to what was wild but with no heart for a wilderness at hand." Some of the traditional art lovers were not amused, but a leading Northwest artist gave me a print of her version of the Elk. It was from a series entitled "Romantic Portland." Curiously enough, neither of us knew the other was working that same middle of the street. It led to a long-time friendship and teaming of poetry and art.

On a recent trip to the Coast we got caught by a *tsunami* warning that caused the town to be evacuated. The stuff of Northwest elan was everywhere. A bartender promptly raised the price of beer by a buck a six-pack. His waitress left her tips on the counter and hit for higher ground in a borrowed car. We heard she didn't even have a driver's license. People loaded kids, pets and belongings into cars. A little boy went by with his bird in a cage. The man with a big house on the hill suddenly acquired a hundred house guests. Sightseers clogged the roads while others partied, prayed or just waited. We spent half the night in a pickup truck, peering out to sea at the bobbing boats and ships that were also waiting for the all clear. Very likely it was different, but also the same, for those on the coasts of Hawaii, Canada and Japan. A rich metaphor. The editors are already getting the poems and stories.

Speaking of publication, visitors to the past few American Booksellers Association conventions have been lavish in praise for the books and periodicals from Northwest presses. Excellent work is coming from small literary houses in Idaho, Seattle, Port Townsend and Portland. The quality of the writing is high, the production outstanding. As one reporter put it, "Eyes are looking west in a way they haven't since the beats came out of California."

We who live and work here are looking around too. Oregon's poet laureate is always on the move to Europe, India, Japan or Singapore. Northwest film-makers are being heard from. Our anti-nuclear activists are strong and articulate. More and more, especially since our political leaders are courting their business, we are feeling the influence of the Pacific Rim nations on our culture. Arriving Asian immigrants bring new thread for an earlier ethnic fabric woven by Finns, Swedes and Irishmen. Literary translation flourishes and flows both ways. The printed word is being enriched by a lot more than a Douglas fir or a sprig of kinnikinnick these days. Our old provincialism, if it ever was that, is fast being eroded.

As an area we have really never been culturally deprived. In addition to that kind of wealth around us, and it is developing all the time, Northwesterners jet around a lot. As a friend told me, "I love going to Europe where everything is older than I am." But she didn't miss a festival or theater season at home, either.

Truly, for those of us who are here by choice, and the convert tends to be more fervent than the cradle-born, this is the most wonderful place on earth. There is room to move around, live independently, and work undisturbed. We'll be happy to be allowed to live out our days in its volcanic dust, road apples and rose petals with all the grace and style we can muster. And with a tip of our big hats to William Shakespeare for:

> Let every eye negotiate for itself,
> and trust no agent.

Richard Hoyt

Photo by Janice Johnson

RICHARD HOYT was born in Hermiston, Oregon and attended schools in Umatilla. He holds degrees from the University of Oregon and the University of Hawaii, where he received his Ph.D. in American Studies. He has served as a counterintelligence agent with Army Intelligence, and has extensive experience as a journalist. He has also been a college professor, most recently at Lewis and Clark College. Since 1980, he has published nine books, some of which have been translated into German, Dutch, and Japanese. Lately he has been traveling in Morocco and Spain, doing research for his newest book, *Siege!*

Distilled in Oregon

Until recently I was better known in New York than in Portland because folks here find it hard to believe anyone could earn a living writing fiction and not be dodging muggers in Brooklyn or Queens. One of the questions most asked of me by Oregonians—with astonishment usually—is why do I live in Portland? The reaction of New Yorkers is the opposite. "You live in Portland? Wow, that must be nice!"

The New Yorkers have got it right, of course. It is nice to live in Portland. Why shouldn't an author live here? Other than the rain, which gets to be a bit much at times, Portland is a civilized place to live. My daughter lives here. There are few titles in New York that I can't find in Powell's Books at 10th and Burnside.

The reason for the question, "Why do I live in Portland?" I suspect, is that the public—especially would-be authors—believe writers have to master various forms of sucking and abasement in order to be published. Since the book publishing industry is centered in New York, according to this theory, aspiring writers have to go there for the required kowtowing; that may be true for actors and artists, but not for authors.

Writing fiction is a solitary profession, not a spectator sport. The notion of writers gathered together in passionate conversation may be charming and colorful, but is hardly necessary for a productive career, and in fact may detract from it; talk doesn't write books, hard work does. Show me somebody who spends all his or her time talking about writing and I'll show you somebody who isn't getting published. The chore, in fact, is to get people to leave you alone.

There are no trade secrets I know of that are somehow possessed by New Yorkers but denied Oregonians, Washingtonians, or Montanans. We all know, one way or another, the qualities possessed by writers we admire: a sense of story; an ear for the way real people talk; a feel for the rhythms and subtleties of the English language; intelligence; the ability to invent; a built-in bullshit detector. The quality of the book is what counts—well mostly—and all that should count.

If I tried to go one-on-one with a publisher to negotiate my contracts, guaranteed I'd get screwed each time out and would probably never have time to write. A smart writer gets himself a good agent to put up with all the manure. My man, Jacques de Spoelberch, knows the pitfalls of Manhattan-speak and the book publishing industry. I think my relationship to Jacques is interesting in itself. He is very un-Pacific Northwest; he has an inherited Belgian title and his French is as fluent as his English. He was president of his class at Princeton; I was once voted as having the best-looking nose in my high school class. As an agent and writer we are rather an odd couple, but over the years we've become good friends. He wants me to succeed for reasons that go beyond his wallet: he's proud of my books and wants to find them the largest readership possible.

With Jacques' kind of support, a writer can work anywhere. What's the point in living in an expensive, dangerous place like New York?

Probably more important than where I live now is where I started. Of all of an author's memories probably none are as formative, evocative, and lasting, as the memories of home in the sense of one's youth. This Freudian baggage has a special claim on the adult imagination; inevitably those memories that are the most persistant and intrusive find their way into a writer's stories. I think there's all kinds of evidence that my youth has influenced my fiction, but nothing that makes me any kind of regional author or part of a "Northwest" school, whatever that is. If place of birth defined a writer, we would be required to assign a geographical label to all authors. Thank heavens we don't.

Although the Pacific Northwest has none of those awful but fascinating tensions of class, race, and repressed sex that has given Southern fiction its distinctive character, there's obviously plenty of material here for writers of mainstream fiction. There seems to be a substantial, and growing number of first-rate authors—my friend Craig Lesley, Ivan Doig, and others—whose primary interest is in the Pacific Northwest and the people who live here. I don't think I belong in that group. I do take great pride in being a farm boy from Umatilla, Oregon, who is able to make a decent living writing literate, sophisticated entertainments.

I could live in McAllen or Miami, and my novels would turn out pretty much the same: the product of a sardonic, if not mordant imagination, given to irony, and inhabiting the territory of satire and black humor. Incidently, I don't think my imagination is skewed or demented; I describe the world as it actually works.

Being an "outsider" is said to be one of the reasons for the successful Southern writers who have invaded the salons of Yankeedom from their agrarian homeland. In this sense I am an "outsider" with an imagination different than that produced by Ivy League schools, urban sophistication, or whatever other backgrounds are expected to produce authors of fiction—although I find such generalizations slightly absurd.

All my heroes—flakey detectives, quirky adventurers, outrageous spies—are my alter-egos. One way or another, they're all versions of an educated, mischievous kid from Umatilla turned professional Walter Mitty. My main man, by whatever name—John Denson, Eddie Perini, Jim Quint, James Burlane—enters battle with a memory that is mine. He knows what it was like to sprint through a blizzard to an outdoor toilet, and to sit there shivering from the below-zero air swirling under his behind. He remembers his father pulling a plow behind a pair of enormous work horses. He remembers the plaintive calling of restless geese on a misty river.

I think I owe a lot of my imagination to my dad. When he was negotiating the swapping of a big bay for a suspicious gelding, say, there I'd be, kicking horse dumplings and listening in on the palaver. When he got together with his old whiskey-making buddies, I got to listen in. He knew how to tell a story. He had a way of slipping in wonderful little details. There was the story of the successfully traded horse who died before its greedy, triumphant new owner got it home, and one where my father, having been caught *en flagrante* with a farmer's wife, had to flee on an unbroken horse that was a hell of a bucker. One of the best was about how my uncle had this brand new Overland filled with kegs of moonshine and was bragging about the car to the captain of a ferry tug when to his horror his handsome automobile rolled into the Columbia River.

The omnipresence of greed, vanity, illusion and delusion, the inevitability of fuckups, the footprints of assholes and posturing fools—those were the themes of Clyde Hoyt's moonshining and horsetrading stories, and they seem to have become mine as well.

My dad once defined manhood for me by saying that boys pee, men piss, the rising of foam signaling arrival. I spent years with strained face and bunched stomach muscles, lacing it to ant hills in order to make the team, yearning for the day when the foam would well up like a head of Guinness. My quirky spy, James Burlane, has a congenitally small bladder and can't make it past two hours, much less make foam; one of these trips almost cost him his life on the Trans-Siberian Express. I have the same problem. In riding that train to research *Head of State*, I found it impossible to void into a plastic bottle while lying on my side and so had to stagger down the car in the middle of the night to relieve myself while standing sleepy-eyed in a lake of Russian urine.

When I was sixteen and driving pea truck, I went to a movie theater in Walla Walla with some friends for some Northeastern Oregon fun. We poured tepid water into bags of hot popcorn and went to the balcony where we made vomiting sounds and dumped the mess onto the unfortunate people who were watching Rock Hudson and Doris Day. When I was forty-three, I wrote a novel in which a dissident Jewish poet—helped by an eccentric spy from Umatilla—steals Comrade Lenin's head from the tomb in Red Square.

When peas were finished, I drove truck in wheat harvest near Pendleton; the hired man had huge boxes filled with mysteries: a lot of Richard S. Prather, Mickey Spillane, and Carter Brown. I used to read two or three a day while waiting for the combine to dump another load of wheat in my truck, or while waiting my turn at the elevator. Was that why I wound up writing thrillers? Possibly.

I once worked on a road crew sealing Interstate-5 through Seattle which could account for me putting my private detective there. But I suspect market appeal, thus greed, had more to do with it. Seattle has a famous architectural phallus and Puget Sound, plus the other trappings of a class city: more serial murderers, rapists and accumulated grief. When John Denson goes to his hometown of Cayuse, Oregon, he goes to Umatilla, where I attended school from the first grade through high school. The cemetery mentioned in *Decoys* was where my maternal grandparents are buried.

In *The Manna Enzyme*, Fidel Castro shaves his beard in the Plaza Hotel—wondering what it would be like to lay Barbara Walters—and goes to Oregon with two of his pals. In Portland, he goes to a disco named Krakatoa Kate's which has nothing to do with Earthquake Ethel's in Beaverton. Finally, he is involved in a shoot-out on the North Umpqua River just south of Diamond Lake. As it happens, my former in-laws live in Roseburg, and I've been up that river many times. In *Siskiyou*, John Denson shoots the rapids below Steamboat on the corpse of a naked girl.

The goose hunting scene that provides the controlling metaphor in *Decoys*, my first novel, is flat-out autobiographical. Sitting there in front of my 1929 Royal, broke as a result of a divorce, determined to write fiction, I remembered how it was. I felt the cold, heard the geese, saw them flying low through the snow, heard their plaintive cries. Such are the contributions of place and detail on the imagination.

But the truth is I'm increasingly becoming an internationalist and will probably be writing fewer John Densons in the future. I traveled to Jamaica and Amsterdam to research *Cool Runnings*; I rode the train across the Soviet Union to research *Head of State*; I lived in Hong Kong and Macao to research my newest book *The Dragon Portfolio*—in which I invented a cunning older brother for Deng Xiaoping; and I'll soon be pushing off for Morocco and Spain to research the Palistinian hijacking of Gilbraltar. After that I plan to write a novel set in northern Australia and New Guinea.

Along the way, I've accumulated a variety of British, Dutch, German, French, Italian, Spanish, Portuguese, and Japanese publishers. Those readers, first charmed by John Denson's adventures in Oregon and Washington, now perceive me as an internationalist and satirist, and they are the source of a substantial portion of my income. Also my thrillers, besides being more complex, are written in the third person, which gives me a chance to hop in and out of a wonderful variety of skins and imaginations. They're harder novels to write, but more fun too.

In a way I'll miss flakey John; in writing his adventures I learned how to tell a story. There is one thing I did find out and that is that readers just love novels set in their back yard. Perhaps I'll write a Denson now and then just to keep touch with my origins.

Having said all of the above about the influence of growing up in Umatilla, I'll admit that it's something of a chore going back to visit. I begin pacing after ten minutes. A New Yorker, with good reason, would surely conclude that Umatilla is one of the most pathetic places imaginable as a place to grow up In retrospect, it seems that way even to me. I'm a different person now. I like bookstores and libraries, and the company of people who read books. I now require traffic jams to swear at and cafes where I can drink coffee with Bohemians and read book reviews and magazines published by colorful British loons.

I've long since moved on from my 1929 Royal. I resigned my tenured slot on the faculty of Lewis and Clark College. Now every morning it's *mano-a-maquina* with the green pit that is the screen of my computer. This is damned hard work, but is not done more easily in Brooklyn than in Beaverton.

I have a theory about the large number of aspiring authors who live in the Pacific Northwest as evidenced by the huge membership of Willamette Writers, and the rapid growth of the Oregon Writers Colony. This is my Alfred T. Mahan theory of creativity in the Pacific Northwest. (You'll recall that Mr. Mahan, among others, concluded that weather is a key to economic productivity, and that overbearing heat and awful humidity is responsible for lethargy in the tropics.) A study recently cited in *Publishers Weekly* reported that the four American cities with the highest number of bookstores per capita were—in no particular order—Austin, San Diego, Seattle, and Portland.

Without speculating on Austin or San Diego, I say the reason for the large number of readers in Portland and Seattle is the miserable rain that often begins in October and remains until June. On a winter day in Minneapolis, a person can step outside and go cross-country skiing or ice-skating. It may be cold, but the sun is out. What do you do if you're a literate, imaginative person, and live west of the Cascades where you can't take a comfortable walk nine months of the year? Well, you read, or you write. Alas, I bet more television is watched also.

Is it really all that amazing that a city the size of Portland, without a major university, is able to support Powell's Books, said to be the largest and most complete bookstore on the West Coast? I don't think so. Just as the *Publishers Weekly* statistics suggest that there are a lot of readers in western Oregon and Washington, it's hardly surprising that there are a lot of authors and would-be authors here too, a cause of celebration and pride.

Does a similar climate at least partly account for the large number of writers in Ireland? If we were able to ban television from western Oregon and Washington, would we give the Irish some competition? I say we do it.

M. K. Wren

Photo by Ann Sullivan

M. K. WREN began studying painting at the age of ten, and began writing at the age of twelve. Daughter of a petroleum geologist and a primary school teacher, Wren grew up in Oklahoma, Kansas, and Texas. After studying both art and writing at the University of Oklahoma, she worked for a year as a designer at Hallmark Cards in Kansas City. Shortly after that she moved to Oregon, where she first worked as a painter. Her first mystery was published by Doubleday in 1973. Since then she has worked steadily and successfully as a writer of both mysteries and science fiction. Her books have been translated into German, Italian, and French. She lives on the Oregon coast.

Out of Amarillo

I was born in Amarillo, Texas.

I've considered using that as an opening line for a story. It's a good hook. It tells the reader a lot about the character. Rather, it suggests a lot, especially to readers who have ever been through Amarillo, Texas. The words conjure up a world and a life experience of such overwhelming bleakness that readers understand immediately that this character has been internally scarred by the experience, that this character is not like other people, that this character is stamped with the desolation of the place and is probably melancholic at the least, or even dangerous.

Of course, there are people who live in Amarillo, Texas who will blithely assure you that they live in "God's Country." I have always assumed that such people are myopic and/or have never set foot out of Amarillo, Texas. Odd, isn't it, that home is so often God's Country. I suppose if your god is the creator of the universe, you can't be wrong, wherever you happen to live.

Actually, Amarillo, Texas is an ordinary, not unpleasant town of about 120,000 people where the streets are named for the Presidents and, when I was there, were paved with brick. Chinese elm, a weedish tree blandly ordinary in appearance, is prevalent along the streets. It is one of the few trees that will grow there. My grandmother had a small lawn of Kentucky bluegrass where as a child I ran barefoot, but such lawns are a time- and water-consuming luxury. Bermuda grass was more commonly planted there. Like the Chinese elm, its leaves are dry and tough. Such lawns are no pleasure for a child's bare feet.

But, as I said, the town is not unusual. What would stamp a character from this place is the town's context. The Llano Estacado; the Staked Plain. The Great Plains. Look at a map of the United States. There are highways that run north from Texas without once curving for hundreds of miles through Kansas, Nebraska, South Dakota, North Dakota, to the Canadian border and beyond. Carl Sandburg said, "There's nothing between Amarillo and the North Pole but a barbed-wire fence." (Actually, he was only quoting a bit of folk wisdom that's probably as old as Amarillo, itself.) The plain is divided with an engineer's passion for right angles into huge fields of grain, or else left to rank, yard-high growth where cattle graze. Nothing breaks the flat horizon except perhaps the pall of smoke from a carbon black plant, a grain elevator, windmill, or occasionally a row of bent Chinese elms planted as a windbreak. You could set out walking from Amarillo, Texas and walk until you died and never see anything different for as long as you were capable of staying on your feet. Except you might run into a dust storm. When I was in high school in Amarillo, Texas, I remember a day that was pitch black at noon. With dust. That's what they call a Black Duster. No, this was not in the Dust Bowl days. In fact, it was in the fifties.

As flat and endless as the sea, but it doesn't move, it doesn't change, the Staked Plain. Change is all in the sky there. The dusters, yes, but there were also magnificent thunderstorms. They are the only things I miss about Amarillo, Texas. For one thing, you could watch those storms coming for a great distance, since nothing impeded your view. And the thunder and lightning were terrifying and exhilarating.

But the land . . . it is all the same, however far you look. There is no variety, no change. And the human mind can't tolerate unchange. Unchange, whatever your situation, pleasant or unpleasant, means boredom, and boredom is the seed of madness. Change and variation are basic to life and to sanity, and writers – contrary to popular opinion – must retain their hold on sanity in order to write.

I remember once as a child traveling with my parents to the nearest mountains, which happened to be the Sangre de Christos in New Mexico. Mountains! Land that changed miraculously at every curve in the road. And roads with *curves*, for that matter. Rugged peaks that even in summer wore patches of snow. And trees. Oh, the trees. Pines like velvet on the mountain flanks, and fields of golden aspen sparkling in the wind. And air that didn't smell of dust and dryness, that was as refreshing to breathe as a double handful of cold, mountain stream water. I was in heaven.

Then we had to go home. To Amarillo, Texas.

There is a point about fifty or sixty miles east of Santa Fe where the highway slips over the shoulder of the last hill, and suddenly you can see before you the plains: the endless, dry, drab, unchanging, unvarying plains. I remember when I saw that vista, I cried.

The human mind hungers for change, for variety.

And my mind hungered for mountains, for trees, for roads that curved.

In the fullness of time, by serendipitous happenchance, I came to Oregon.

And I found everything that I had longed for here, and something that I had never dared even hope for: the sea.

I came, by a stroke of incredible luck, to live in Oregon *by the sea*.

I look out my window at this moment at the Pacific Ocean, and my life is pervaded by the sound of it. It is profoundly constant, the sea, in that it is never from one day, one hour, or one minute to the next the same.

I am in heaven.

There is, of course, the little problem of making a living. This piece of land on which my heaven exists is not, like the sea-cleansed air I breathe, free.

But I'm a writer, and one can write anywhere. Possibly even in Amarillo, Texas. And any writer who couldn't write in this setting is in trouble, and any writer whose writing would be unaffected by this setting is numb from the neck up. My context pervades my writing like the sound of the sea pervades my life. I can't escape either, and I can't imagine wanting to escape them.

I've written six mystery novels, and my series character detective, Conan Flagg, lives in a house by the sea, as I do (although his is much fancier than mine), and he owns an old book shop, and, not coincidentally, I once worked in the old Lincoln Book Shop in what was then Nelscott. I designed Conan as a series character and gave him the money, time, and psychological attributes that would make it possible for him to solve crimes anywhere in the world. Yet in six novels, he has traveled outside the boundaries of Oregon only once. That was when he went to Silver City, Idaho, which got him about fifty miles over the Oregon state line. Will Conan eventually travel to faraway exotic places as I originally planned? I really don't think so. He is too much at home in Oregon.

Besides, exotic is in the eye of the beholder.

One of my mystery novels was set in Harney County, in southeastern Oregon, and it was the first of my books to be sold to an Italian publisher. My editor told me the Italians love exotic settings. Like Harney County.

The English, Germans, and French apparently love my exotic

settings, too. I can understand that now. I've lived long enough—over twenty years—in this exotic setting to realize how rare it is in a world so crowded with people, so devastated by their presence and demands.

Yes, I know there are other places in the world that share some of the qualities of this region, that are scenic and, in some cases, even more untouched by human hands, that are equally various. I'm happy in the knowledge that such places exist, and equally happy to let them exist without experiencing them firsthand. I have more than enough to keep me occupied for as long as I live within a few hour's or day's drive north, east, or south.

Does that have the ring of smug provincialism in it? Am I saying I live in God's Country and meaning that the rest of the world is unworthy of deific attention?

No, I'm just saying that I was born in Amarillo, Texas, where change and variation are nonexistent, or at best subtle, and I have found myself miraculously transported like Dorothy and Toto to a place of continual change and astounding variation, and I will never cease to be amazed at it, and will never in my lifetime be able to explore and know all its aspects.

This land constantly surprises me. Rainforests at this latitude surprised me when I first discovered them. So did the High Desert lying in the rain shadow of the Cascades, and the stark, lean Basin and Range country of southeastern Oregon. Even places I think I know well surprise me. The light shifts, the shadows elucidate new shapes; the tide floods the beach to our seawall, ebbs to lay bare the rippled floor of the sea; sand accumulates in drifting barchans six feet deep on the summer beach, and winter storms sweep the beach clean to bedrock; at the first sign of spring, alders veil themselves in pink—not green; in autumn, vine maples burn exquisitely like displaced bonsais in their lush, dark settings; snow turns a green and gold mountain forest into hushed gray and white within minutes, lies deep and downy on the cobbles of a stream where it is sculpted into Brancusi curves by the water; a rainstorm in the High Desert retreats behind a rainbow, and the scent of the rain-wet sage is intoxicating; and in a small basin palisaded with basalt, I find a ring of rocks placed there—by Piutes, probably—when the creek bed nearby still rang with rushing water where sand blows now with the fallen leaves of stunted aspen. And occasionally, a mountain explodes.

But all this is just *setting*, right? Background. Scenery. Fiction isn't about places. It's about people.

Right. But people cannot be separated from their context, and another thing that surprises me about this country is the variation in its people. I realize that Oregon is not as varied in its racial and ethnic mix, as say, New York City. But the whole state has only about a quarter of the population of that one city. And Oregon's relatively sparse population exists in a wondrously various setting. This land sifts people out and deposits them where they can survive, and it provides a broad spectrum of niches for individuals. Like all fiction, my stories are about people, but people are shaped by and sometimes inseparable from their setting. One of the ideals toward which I strive in my writing is to create characters who could only exist in the setting in which I place them. My characters are derived from their context, and their context is *my* context.

Yes, I have written a science fiction novel that has truly exotic settings, including a couple of hypothetical planets of the star Alpha Centauri B. Yet those imaginary settings are rooted ultimately in my setting, in the extraordinary variety of it. And the book I'm writing now, which is also science fiction of sorts, is set in the locale with which I am most familiar: the central Oregon coast. I can't seem to escape my own setting in my writing, and I don't intend to try. This country—and the sea—feeds my senses, and my senses feed my mind, and that's where stories come from.

My own setting is not indestructible, of course, and in fact some aspects of it are very fragile. My awareness of its vulnerability is a shadow on my existence. I, who longed for changeableness, do not want this country to change—not if change means destruction. My attitude is, now that I'm here, close the gates. And don't mess it up. Don't change a thing.

A selfish attitude, no doubt, but I have found *my* God's Country, and I don't think I could exist in any other setting any more than my characters could.

I'm not a native Northwesterner. I'm an immigrant. What that means is that I've paid my dues. I've made my home the old-fashioned way: I've *earned* it. And it is mine, all mine, now. It is in my bones, in every cell of my body, and my every thought is shaped by it.

You native sons and daughters of the Northwest—I hope you know what you have here. I was born in Amarillo, Texas, and I know.

William Kittredge

Photo by Geoffrey J. Sutton

WILLIAM KITTREDGE was raised in the Warner Rim area of Eastern Oregon. Since 1969 he has taught at the University of Montana, where he is now Professor of Creative Writing. He held a Stegner Fellowship at Stanford University, and has been awarded two grants from the National Endowment for the Arts. Two collections of short stories have brought him the Fiction International Award, the Montana Governor's Award for Literature, and the Pacific Northwest Bookseller's Award for Excellence. With co-editor Steven Krauzer, Kittredge has produced anthologies for the New American Library, for TriQuarterly and for Harper and Row. He has co-written a series of westerns, and won the Neil Simon Award for his work on the film *Heartland*.

New to the Country

In July of 1969 I came to Montana to stay, bearing a new Master of Fine Arts degree from the flooding heartland of Iowa. I had just finished up as a thirty-five-year-old, in-off-the-ranch graduate student in the Writers Workshop, and I had lucked into a teaching job at the University of Montana. I was running to native cover in the West; I was a certified writer, and this was the beginning of my real life at last.

During that summer in Iowa City – drinking too much, in love with theories about heedlessness and possibility – I was trying to figure out how to inhabit my daydream. We lived in an old stone-walled house with a flooded basement out by the Coralville reservoir, listening to cockroaches run on the night-time linoleum and imagining Montana, where we would find a home.

Every morning the corn in the fields across the road looked to have grown six inches, every afternoon the skies turned green with tornado-warning storms, and every night lightning ran magnificent and terrible from the horizons. My wife said they ought to build a dike around the whole damned state of Iowa and turn it into a catfish preserve. The U-Haul trailer was loaded. After a last party we were history in the Midwest, gone to Montana, where we were going to glow in the dark.

The real West started at the long symbolic interstate bridge over that mainline to so many ultimately heart-breaking American versions of heaven, the Missouri River. Out in the middle of South Dakota I felt myself released into significance. It was clear I was aiming my life in the correct direction. We were headed for a town studded with abandoned teepee burners.

But moreso – as we drove I imagined Lewis and Clark and Catlin and Bodmer and even Audubon up to Fort Union on the last voyage of his life in 1843, along with every wagon train, oxcart, cattle drive, and trainload of honyockers, all in pursuit of that absolute good luck which is some breathing time in a commodious place where the best that can be is right now. In the picture book of my imagination I was seeing a Montana composed of major postcards. The great river sliding by under the bridge was rich with water from the Sun River drainage, where elk and grizzly were rumored to be on the increase.

Engrossed in fantasies of traveling upriver into untouched territory, I was trying to see the world fresh, as others had seen it. On April 22, 1805, near what is now the little city of Williston in North Dakota, Meriwether Lewis wrote:

> . . . immence herds of Buffaloe, Elk, deer, & Antelopes feeding in one common and boundless pasture. we saw a number of bever feeding on the bark of the trees along the verge of the river, several of which we shot, found them large and fat.[1]

By 1832, at the confluence of the Missouri and the Yellowstone, the painter George Catlin was already tasting ashes while trying to envision a future—just as I was trying to imagine what had been. Catlin wrote:

> . . . the native Indian in his classic attire, galloping his wild horse, with sinewy bow, and shield and lance, amid the fleeting herds of elks and buffaloes. What a beautiful and thrilling specimen for America to preserve and hold up to the view of her refined citizens and the world, in future ages! A *nation's park*, containing man and beast, in all the wild and freshness of their nature's beauty![2]

Think of Audubon responding eleven years later, on May 17, 1843, in that same upriver country around Fort Union:

> Ah! Mr. Catlin, I am now sorry to see and to read your accounts of the Indians *you* saw—how very different they must have been from any that I have seen![3]

On July 21, Audubon wrote:

> What a terrible destruction of life, as it were for nothing, or next to it, as the tongues only were brought in, and the flesh of these fine animals was left to beasts and birds of prey, or to rot on the spots where they fell. The prairies are literally *covered* with the skulls of the victims . . . .[4]

On August 5, Audubon finished the thought:

> But this cannot last; even now there is a perceptible

difference in the size of the herds, and before many years the Buffalo, like the Great Auk, will have disappeared; surely this should not be permitted.[5]

In our summer of 1969 we poked along the edge where the Badlands break so suddenly from the sunbaked prairies, imagining the faraway drumming of hooves, Catlin's warriors on their decorated horses coming after us from somewhere out of dream. Not so far south lay Wounded Knee.

We studied the stone faces of our forefathers at Mount Rushmore and didn't see a damned thing because by that time in the afternoon we were blinded by so much irony on a single day. We retired for the night to a motel somewhere south of the Devil's Post Pile in Wyoming. I was seeing freshly, but not always what I hoped to see. The distances were terrifying.

By the time we reached Missoula, I had disassociated my sensibilities with whiskey, which gave me the courage to march up the concrete steps to Richard Hugo's house, only a block from the Clark Fork River, where the Village Inn Motel sits these days. I rapped on his door. He studied me a moment after I introduced myself. "You're very drunk," he said.

Well hell, I thought, now you've done it.

"Wait a minute," Hugo said. "I'll join you."

Home, I thought, childlike with relief. This was the new country I had been yearning for, inhabited by this man who smiled and seemed to think I should be whatever I could manage.

That particular pilgrimage started years before. Like so many of the students at the University of Montana, those who have grown up rural and so seemingly isolated from anything our national media culture defines as significant, I felt myself cut off from the so-called Great World in irrevocable ways. So many of us in the West feel deprived and driven to the contrary idea that the things we know are worthless, or at least of no interest to anybody else, because they are so private. Dick Hugo helped us disabuse ourselves of such notions.

In the far outback of high desert basin and range country where I was a young man, a land-locked peat-ground valley just north of the Nevada state line in southeastern Oregon, we lived a long way from bookstores. And I believed myself ruined for this isolation by my dumbfounded discovery of books and ideas, nodding my head in dimwitted agreement with Camus, terrified by *The Magic Mountain*, subscribing to *The New York Times Book Review*, the *Kenyon Review*, the *Sewanee Review*, the *Hudson Review*, and the *Virginia Quarterly Review*, ordering eight or ten deeply serious books a month long distance from San Francisco—occasionally a good one—hungering at the meager collections shelved in stationery stores when I got to town, twenty-six years old, home from some years in Strategic Air Command intelligence on Guam, a grown man with family, ill-educated and close to paralyzed by my inability to want any life I could imagine as possibly mine. My yearnings seemed almost perverse. Why couldn't the immediacy of family and work and property be enough?

How right and ironic it seemed that afternoon in Shaw's Stationery in Klamath Falls, as I leafed through a recent reissue of *Oregon Place Names* and found the name Lonely. It turned out to be the former name of Adel in Warner Valley, the place where I had been raised and was living right at the moment. Not one thing about such a sappish discovery loomed comic at that time in my life.

Eventually I made other finds in Shaw's Stationery—Theodore Roethke's *Collected Poems*, for one—and I read in "The Far Field":

> Among the tin cans, tires, rusted pipes,
> broken machinery,—
> One learned of the eternal[6]

The poem goes on to talk about dead rats and tomcats and ground beetles amid named, specific flowers and birds, referring to Roethke's childhood wanderings amid his father's greenhouses in Michigan, but I was transfixed right there in Klamath Falls. Roethke's experience in some back corner was valuable if only because he cherished it in such accurate language, and mine might be, someday, maybe. In any event, I recognized chances I had to take but could not name in Roethke, and about then began another version of my life, a story to tell myself and live by. So to hell with lonely, I'll just be whatever it is I can't quit. Another romance with myself, as if they all weren't.

By early October of those years in the early 1960s our four old John Deere 36 combines had been dragged into a row out behind the Caterpillar shop. The light over the harvested barley fields would come up golden and clean for a couple of dozen perfect days.

The great fault-block of Warner Rim lifted three thousand feet just at our backs, marked in long terraces by the remnants of rocky shoreline left behind as some ancient sea dried up. A few miles north, along a thin curve of peninsula reaching out into a shallow floodwater lake, we had found chipped obsidian arrow-points by the bucketful when I was a child. The native peoples must have camped there on these same kinds of limitless fall days, awaiting the calling, undulating rafts of waterbirds and the good hunting. In my imagination those people were absolutely quiet and at peace with their intentions. For them, things had always been like this.

Archaeologists know of a quarter-million points picked up along the shores of Crump Lake, and kids in the country, like me, had a hundred or two stored in a shoebox somewhere. In seasons when the water was low we would wander amid the shredding expanses of dry tule and find the points in clusters of a dozen or more. At the end, people were out there with shovels and screens, like miners, determined to reap their share of whatever bounty they imagined this was. I knew a man who had a half dozen horseshoe nail kegs filled with arrowheads in his garage.

By the early 1960s, the shore of Crump Lake felt too lonesome for anybody in my spiritual condition. The afternoons there didn't seem inhabited any more. But south along the thread of gravel road there were huge smooth-sided boulders etched with lichen growing along the traces of dim pictograph drawings, snakes and sunrises, figures of animals and men, perhaps drawn there in acts of celebration or supplication. Who could know? In any event, the boulders were a truckload each, and nobody had carried them away to a garage. On those fine October days I would study those drawings and wonder what it could have been like to be native in that place where I felt so distant from any hint of proper purpose.

Several hundred feet up the scree slopes, along the terraced rocky lines that marked the shores of that ancient sea, there were caves at the foot of the occasional layered lava-rock outcroppings. Nobody I knew had ever climbed up to them, likely because our energies in that valley went mostly to work, and sweating up some scree slope towards those unimpressive thin lines of shadow looked to be such a thunderingly pointless thing to do. But anybody could see that those old hunting-gathering people who painted their designs on the boulders along the road might have sheltered themselves up there, and I was looking for somebody to be. Maybe I could be an intellectual rancher who did bookish things like archaeology on the side.

Such are the stories we tell ourselves. I didn't know anybody like that, but I entertained thoughts of buying the weekly newspaper over in the county seat and being the rancher/newspaper guy who wrote a fascinating column every week with cowshit on his boots. As I say, I was twenty-six and ruined for the country generosities of the life I had inherited. A good crop of barley was in the bin that fall, and it wasn't enough. So I climbed up to the caves, packing a No. 2 irrigating shovel.

From that elevation, through the stillness of October, I gazed out across the valley we mostly owned. It was so clearly demarcated by what I think of as our own etchings, our ways of making the world captured and sensible: the green geometric patternings of the high irrigation ditches and dragline drainage canals leading to the pumps, the yellow fields of stubble we had so recently harvested, the fencelines where I could have been stalking ring-necked pheasant that afternoon. But I didn't spend much time contemplating the vista. If there was anything I knew by heart, it was the configurations of that property.

The rough, sloping roof over the mouth of the shallow cave was black and encrusted, and I had read enough to guess what that meant—soot and animal fats, a long history of cook fires, maybe over centuries. My theories were right; people had sheltered themselves here. I was truly and immediately excited, my hands trembling as I envisioned some great simple goldfield find, trying to put aside my fantastical notions of who I would be now that such impossible bonanza luck had come my way.

What I remember next is the shoveling, there in the mounded rubble at the mouth of the cave, where I had room to stand and work while fighting back the feeling that this was make-believe and not part of my actual life at all. Since the end of harvest I had been searching, unconsciously or not, seeking signs and omens to kick me forward into the process of creating a story of who I should be. Those that I acknowledged had brought me to this hillside above the place where I had always lived, digging for buried secrets. It was a scenario my cattle rancher friends might understand as quite literally indicative of craziness. And more than anything I was terrified that they might be right about someone so unmoored from the routines of normal life as it was supposed to be lived in our valley.

But before long my shoveling turned up a reward that at first I could not make sense of—a fragment of fine matting woven from rushes. It seemed impossible that the people who drew those slapstick marks on the boulders below could have known how to work so intricately with materials so commonplace in the valley. But connections started forming.

A few miles away, on the flat-topped lava outcroppings along the eastern side of the valley, there were smooth cylindrical holes worn maybe ten or fifteen inches into the fundamental stone by Modoc or Shoshoni or Klamath natives grinding the native grains. The holes are like bowls, and once worked into the outcropping they could not be destroyed by enemies. Whatever tribe it was and how many thousands of hours at the grinding it took to wear those holes no one knows; but for me, like the crumbling woven mat, that stone worn to the shape of the work came to exist as metaphor.

There in the mouth of my shallow cave I realized my connection to the unimagined continuities of life in the place where I lived. It was an instant that cannot help but sound soft-headed in the recounting—you cannot describe the ineffable, you have to trigger readers into imagining it for themselves—but I now think of it as a quite classical instant of recognition, in which I began to sense in the most inarticulate of ways the legitimacy of my urge to tell stories.

Over the next weeks and months, what had been a slowly accumulating intention began to become resolve. On the day after Thanksgiving in 1965, when I was thirty-three years old, I started writing stories that I have learned to understand as useful, if they are ever useful, precisely as that broken bit of woven matting and those bowls worn in the fundamental stone were useful to me, as gestures passing from one person to another.

* * *

A mythology can be understood as a story that contains a set of implicit instructions from a society to its members, telling them what is valuable and how to conduct themselves if they are to preserve the things they value. In the American West, we are struggling to revise our dominant mythology, a story called The Western, hoping to see through to the so-called Real West. In essence, we are trying to find a new story to inhabit.

The struggle is of extraordinary importance. Our laws control our lives, and they are designed to preserve a model of society based on values learned from our mythology. Only after reimagining our myths can we remodel our laws and hope to keep our society in a realistic relationship to what is actual.

It is important to understand that the mythology of the American West is the most central mythology of our nation and that it is a part of a much older world myth, the myth of law-bringing. Which means it is a mythology of conquest.

The story begins with a vast innocent continent, natural and almost magically alive, capable of inspiring us to reverence and awe, and yet savage – a wilderness. The story goes on to a pastoral people who come from the East, bringing law and civilization. But the law does not command much respect from the original inhabitants of the land, who after all had laws of their own to respect. The law does not always command much respect even from those who bring it. People seeking frontiers are often people seeking escape from law, bringing terrible demons with them – lust and greed for property and power and that ultimate abstraction, which is money.

Our good pastoral people are often, because they are law-abiding, too weak to enforce their laws and need help, which comes in the form of a magical hero – the good warrior from the sacred and innocent wilds who possesses wilderness skills and the existential knowledge that it is sometimes necessary to kill, to be essentially lawless in the service of law and order. This hero saves our people from the savage forces of lust and greed. He alone has the magical wilderness speed of hand and the willingness to kill. And he has the sad knowledge of his responsibilities. His knowledge is sad because he has to go away after he is finished with the killing, back to the mythological wilderness. His willingness to embrace violence, even in the service of law, is a disruptive force in society. He is a killer in a society that cannot endorse violence. He does our dirty work, then carries our guilt away with him, leaving us to go about the business of our days with clean hands and souls.

This is our great paradoxical, problematic American teaching story. It is also the plot of *Shane*. It is a story as ancient as the problem of law and law-bringing.

The holy and innocent hero comes from the wilderness and slays the dragon that is threatening society, then rides away like a movie star. An obvious societal good has been served by the violence of an outsider. The story is as old as settlements and invading armies and deeply problematic because it is at the heart of a racist, sexist, imperialist mythology of conquest. It is a rationale for violence, against other people and against nature. It is The Western, a morality play that was never much acted out anywhere in the "Real West." Or anywhere.

The actual West was no doubt violent at times, but never so obsessed with killing as our story would have us imagine. Nobody would have been left alive. More people have been killed in Missoula in the last few weeks than in Dodge City in its heyday. Certainly the West was not much traveled by holy gunfighters engaged in the business of setting things right.

At the same time, that mythology is a lens through which we continue to see ourselves. Many of us like to imagine ourselves as honest, pastoral yeomen who sweat and work in the woods or the mines or the fields for a living. And many of us are. We live in a real family, a work-centered society, and we like to see ourselves as people with the good luck and sense to live in a place where some remnant of the natural world still exists in working order. Many of us hold that natural world to be sacred in some degree, just as it is in our myth. Lately, more and more of us are coming to understand our society in the American West as an exploited colony, threatened by greedy outsiders who want to take our sacred place away from us, or at least strip and degrade it beyond sacredness.

In short, we see ourselves as a working society of mostly decent people who live in some connection to a holy wilderness, threatened by those who lust for power and property. We look for Shane to come riding out of the Tetons, and we see Exxon and the Sierra Club. One looks about as alien as the other.

Our mythology tells us we own the West, absolutely and morally; we own it because of our history. Our people brought law to this difficult place; they suffered and they shed blood and they survived, and they earned this land for us. The myth tells us this place is ours, and will always be ours, to do with as we see fit.

That's a most troubling and enduring message, because we so want to believe it — and we do believe it, so many of us, despite the ironies and wrongheadedness involved, despite the fact that we took this place from someone else. We try to ignore a genocidal history of violence against the Native Americans.

The truth is, we never owned all the land and water, and we don't even own very much of it, privately. And we don't own anything absolutely or forever. As our society grows more and more complex and interwoven, our title is less and less absolute, more and more likely to be diminished legally. Our rights to property will never take precedence over the needs of society. Nor should they, we all must agree in our grudging heart of hearts. Ownership of property has always been a privilege, granted by society and revokable.

So we find that our mythology, the story by which our society is ordered, has been telling us an enormous lie, and we are mortally angered by the deception. My father grew up on a homestead place on the sagebrush flats outside Silver Lake, Oregon. He tells of hiding under the bed with his sisters when strangers came to the gate. He grew up believing that the one sure defense against the world was property, as we all did in that country and era.

By the time he was thirty-five, my grandfather had bought the cattle ranch in Warner Valley, where I grew up. We summered our cattle on Taylor Grazing Land, where we owned most of the water there was, and it was ours. The government was as distant as news on the radio.

Outside work was done mostly by men and horses and mules, and our ranch valley was filled with life. But we went to tractors and drained the swamps and plowed the tule marshes and draglined the sloughs and bought more machinery and made our way around the corner into agribusiness. The valley went deader and deader as the years passed and our fields were scaled to work, and the work scaled to machinery.

By the time I was old enough to run the farming we had miles of canals and hundreds of redwood headgates, eighteen-inch electric pumps—the works. The most intricate part of my job was called "balancing water," a night-and-day process of opening and closing pipes and running pumps. That system was the finest and most intricate plaything I ever had.

Despite the mud and endless hours, the work remained play for a long time, the perfecting of that irrigation system a kind of artistry, the making of a thing both functional and elegant. That's how we thought of it; we were bringing order to the world, doing God's work and creating a good place on earth, living the pastoral yeoman dream. Our work surely earned us the right to absolute control over the thing we had created.

So you can imagine our surprise and despair, our sense of having been profoundly cheated, when things began to go wrong. We wanted to build a reservoir and litigation started. Our laws were being used against us by people who wanted a share of what we thought of as our water. As the fieldwork became more and more mechanical, we couldn't hire anyone who cared enough to do it right. The peat ground we had drained began to go saline. The waterbirds stopped coming in the great rafts we had so loved to hunt. Instead of creating a great good place, we were destroying our natural oasis. We had lived the right lives, according to mythology, and the mythology had lied. Or the world had proven too complex, the myth too simple-minded.

The myth had told us to bring order to nature, and our order had proven deadly; nature would not fit our industrial model, and we could not endure the boredom of our mechanical work. We killed off the coyotes, and rodents destroyed our alfalfa. We sprayed Parathion for clover mite and shortened our own lives. We started with a sanctuary and ended with a landscape organized like a machine for growing crops and fattening cattle, a machine that creaked a little louder each year, a dreamland gone wrong. We had shaped our piece of the West according to the model provided by our mythology: we had brought it to order, and such order had given us enormous power over nature—a blank perfection of fields—and nature had died.

All over the West, as in all of America, the old story is dying. We find ourselves weathering a rough winter of discontent, snared in the uncertainties of a transitional time and urgently yearning to inhabit a story that might bring sensible order to our lives, even as we know such a story can only evolve through an almost literally infinite series of recognitions of what we hold sacred, individual by individual. If we're lucky, it might be a story that teaches us to abhor our old romance with conquest and progress so that we might revere the particular, where, as Roethke said, "One learned of the eternal."

What I am working toward is an idea of history as a kind of storytelling that triggers our imaginations into the vital act of seeing freshly into the patterns of our lives, both private and public.

Artists help us recognize ourselves. It's their job. We are lucky in

Montana, because we have a tradition of vivid and useful storytelling— *The Journals of Lewis and Clark* and *The Big Sky, Wolf Willow, Wind from an Enemy Sky, A River Runs Through It, Winter in the Blood, This House of Sky*—make your own list.

Making Sure It Goes On, the Collected Poems of Richard Hugo heads mine. Dick loved to drive Montana, his trips imaginative explorations into other lives as a way toward focusing on his own complexities. He made the game of seeing into art, and his poetry and life form a story that lies rock bottom in my understanding of what art is for.

Once we drove over to fish the Jefferson River on a summer day when we were both hung-over to the point of insipid visionary craziness. We didn't catch any fish, and I came home numb, simply spooked; but Dick saw some things and wrote a poem called "Silver Star."

Each time I read "Silver Star" I rediscover an implied story about homes, and the courage to acknowledge such a need, a story about Dick and his continual refinding of his own life, an instruction about storytelling as the art of constructing road maps, ways home to that ultimate shelter that is the coherent self. It's a gift. Montana is a landscape reeking with such conjunction and resonance. They fill the silence.

Not long ago, on a bright spring morning, I stood on the cliffs of the Ulm Pishkun where the Blackfeet drove dusty hundreds of bison to fall and die. Gazing east I could dimly see the great Anaconda Company smokestack there on the banks of the Missouri like a finger pointing to heaven above the old saloon-town city of Great Falls where Charlie Russell painted and traded his pictures for whiskey, only a little upstream from the place where Meriwether Lewis wrote, having just finished an attempt at describing his first sight of the falls:

> after writing this imperfect discription I again viewed the falls and was so much disgusted with the imperfect idea which it conveyed of the scene that I determined to draw my pen across it and begin agin, but then reflected that I could not perhaps succeed better . . . .[7]

After so many months of precise notation, all in the service of Thomas Jefferson's notion of the West as useful, in one of the most revealing passages written about the American West, Lewis seems to be saying: *But this, this otherness is beyond the capture of my words, this cannot be useful, this is dream.* The dam-builders, of course, did not see it his way.

Behind me loomed the fortress of the rock-sided butte Charlie Russell painted as backdrop to so much history, with the Rockies off beyond on the western horizon, snowy and gleaming in the morning sun. This listing could go on, but I was alone and almost frightened by so many conjunctions visible at once, and so many others right down the road: the Gates of the Mountains and Last Chance Gulch and even make-believe—Boone Caudill and Teal Eye and Dick Summers over west on the banks of the Teton River where it cuts through the landscapes of *The Big Sky*—history evident all around and the imaginings of artists and storytellers intertwined. Charlie Russell and Bud Guthrie and Dick Hugo and Meriwether Lewis created metaphoric territory as real as any other Montana in the eye of my imagination.

We all play at imagining ourselves into history, new to the country, seeing freshly, reorienting ourselves and our schemes within the complexities of the world. It is a powerful connection to history, and the grand use we make of storytelling as we incessantly attempt to recognize that which is sacred and the point of things.

Notes

1. From *The Journals of Lewis and Clark*, edited by Bernard DeVoto, Boston: Houghton Mifflin Co., 1953.

2. Quoted in Frank Bergon, editor, *The Wilderness Reader*, New York: New American Library, 1980.

3. John James Audubon, *Audubon and His Journals*, edited by Maria R. Aububon, Vol. 1, New York: Dover, 1960.

4. From *Audubon and His Journals*, Vol. 2.

5. From *Audubon and His Journals*, Vol. 2.

6. From "The Far Field," *The Collected Poems of Theodore Roethke*, Garden City, New York: Anchor Press, 1975. Reprinted by permission from The Far Field, c 1962, by Beatrice Roethke, Administratrix of the Estate of Theodore Roethke. From the Collected Poems of Theodore Roethke. Published by Doubleday and Co., Inc.

7. From *The Journals of Lewis and Clark*.

Laura Jensen

Photo by Janet Ness

LAURA JENSEN holds a Master of Fine Arts degree from the University of Iowa Writers Workshop. For the past twelve years she has lived in the historic district of Tacoma, the same town her mother's large family grew up in. She has traveled throughout the United States to visit and give readings and workshops. In the years since 1972, she has published eight books and chapbooks of poems, the most recent book is titled *Shelter*, and published by Dragon Gate, Inc. Her writing has also been supported by grants from the National Endowment for the Arts, and the Ingram Merrill Foundation.

Stars and Streetlights

In the photographs the children wade and row and swim. They ride from Old Tacoma to Vashon Island in a small inboard called the Serena. They have permission to camp on the beach. The whole family stays. I think I need to know the evergreens myself to know colors and shadows and sounds of birds. The photographs of my mother and her brothers camping on Vashon Island may date from 1918 or '19 or the early twenties.

Summers we visited my great-uncles' small house. There was a garden, and my uncle was a caretaker at Docton State Park. They had a Siamese cat and a chicken house with terrifying red chickens. My uncle cared for his brother, who was a diabetic in a wheelchair. I was a Scandinavian child changing into my swimsuit in the paneled bathroom. I knew Scandinavian children would not have to wear swimsuits. It was dark and cool in the living room with leathery blue chairs and *Readers Digest* condensed books. My uncles listened to Swedish language programs on the radio. We left the secluded little house to walk just down the road and path to the rocky beach. When I was twelve or so my uncle in the wheelchair passed away and the caretaker uncle returned to Sweden. I watched from the airport window as he carried his SAS bag to the plane. It was exciting that he would fly over the pole. Sweden had always waited for him to come home. But it was sad that he would not live here any longer. Just last year he passed away at ninety-nine.

I have not known myself as a regional person, but as a child I knew the water, evergreens, pebbles, shells, seaweed, and knew ferries were a part of that. The island or the beach was not too far away. I could ride a bike to Vashon Island, a friend asked me to visit her beach place, the park with the ferry landing had a beach and woods. When I graduated from high school I was asked on a day trip on a yacht. We toured past McNeil Island where people lived without benefits or privileges. These people are very real. Tomas Transtromer wrote, "Perhaps letting the truth escape from books would help./ We have to go farther . . ./ Those who are ahead have a long way to go."[1] My truth about that day trip: it was a leap beyond privilege to luxury. The yacht was beautiful, but I was not—I was human. But I felt graced there, and none of the others allowed me to feel sorry that my upbringing was not filled with luxury, that the trip was a departure from my own reality.

We are a society of automobiles. As a poet that frightens me, and I acknowledge that I am a member of that society—I accept rides with friends, I have my instant coffee and box of cereal. But as an undergraduate my walk from the University of Washington to my rooming house took me through a parking lot. Once there were trees, then I passed metal and glass. At the end of the lot I often felt stunned by glitter, and I have remembered a headachy nausea. I still see that glittering snake at rest in my mind, the snake I see on the I-5 corridor. Now when I ride the bus I am surprised by a feeling that single drivers in machines of such weight and force cannot make a rational truth. This feeling may come from my privilege to have met a Northwest island or to know poetry or both.

The poetry I have read has taught me that our existence in nature is a paradox. Twenty years ago I began work at a branch library as a page. (Through the last two years of high school I was on my way to work or coming home during the national news hour, I missed the Vietnam war coverage completely.) I discovered a book by David Wagoner. I was writing my own poems. As a freshman I studied with David Wagoner, then Mark Strand and Galway Kinnell, and once or twice took the ferry from Seattle to walk on Vashon Island, carrying notebook and pencils. Once a motorcyclist on a logging road slowed and paralleled my steps for far too long. After my graduate school years at the University of Iowa I returned to Tacoma, but have continued to read American poetry and essays, also some feminist poetry and feminist essays. I am not influenced exclusively by Northwest poetry. However, David Wagoner works closely with the Northwest landscape, and his influence in spirit has been real to me for twenty years. Feminism seems no denial of poetry, and it affects my feelings about natural places by adding fervor.

But "Emotions cannot be verified nor aspirations proved," says a fortune cookie. This means these are abstractions, and even concrete action that represents an emotion or aspiration cannot make an abstraction real. My feelings about the necessity for conservation have not inspired me. As poets we recreate our environment in words, but for me poetry has no motive beyond the making.

2.

My earliest experience with metaphor was words that formed as I gazed at beauty in nature. I think the same thread followed for twenty years. When I ask myself if my experience has changed, if my remembrance of the composition of my earliest poems seems to differ from poems I write now, I have no answer. From a Greyhound coming into Port Angeles: before the water was a tide basin or lagoon where a deer passed through in high grass, by the road was a table that displayed shells from large to small and someone in shorts and shirt who guarded the table and suntanned. I wondered about a poem called "She Sells Sea Shells by the Sea Shore." This tongue-twister coming to mind underlined for me that poets see and words happen.

A walk on the beach is a visit now, but it recalls the earlier understanding I drew to myself of the area. The memories can be very clear. But the northwest where I spend my life is the kind of neighborhood I knew when I was a child. The blocks have one difference—the architecture of the historic area has a strong identity I love. Closer to the water view are large old homes where the wealthy lived in Old Tacoma. Some are private homes, some are converted to apartments. I have rented rooms in two such buildings.

The first was large and ornate, in good repair, but it housed the less wealthy—single teachers, divorced or unwed mothers, people recovering from illness. Now I live in a smaller converted house. Ninth Street beside it was a skid road, logs were skidded down to the mills on the bay. The landlord is proud to be a member of the Colville Tribe. He tells of finding old photographs in the attic when he bought the house. It was owned by an early educator. Before World War II, two sisters lived there, one a college professor, one a doctor of Christian Science. I find the history in old city directories.

Winters are lifeless after Christmas decorations come down. But I like warmth returning and a sense of renewal each spring. I do not know the neighbors, but find, as in a Randall Jarrell poem, I meet their pets. I also meet their trees. In the telephone book this corner is on the map of downtown Tacoma. I hear sirens each day, jets from the Army or McChord Air Force Base, or airliners cross low.

At the optician's the other day, in a wildlife magazine, I saw that

30 x 40 feet of yard could be registered with the U.S. government as a wildlife preserve.[2] I wondered if plans for a regional library which will expand the library that I worked in during high school could include such a preserve; then I realized planners would point out that a parking lot was necessary. Although it is also true that such a well-visited place might not be ideal for wildlife, still schools and libraries combined with wildlife preserves make sense. It is clear that a neighborhood can work like such a preserve. Woodpeckers, cedar waxwings, evening grosbeaks visit here, and crows and gulls and robins and swallows. Squirrels live in some trees, moths come in summer, once an Aholibah Underwing. I walk a few blocks and see Commencement Bay or look out one window when there are no leaves and see Mount Rainier; and wildlife enters my poems as it comes, from the corner of the eye of life, while it travels through or makes its living.

Despite my understanding that an urban poet is also a Northwest poet – a poet who writes of the inner city and the highway – I think a belief in the natural world is a part of the poet. I think every poet feels concern and dissatisfaction. A tie with nature creates a concern that it remain, and it creates a view of the expanding population and accompanying industry as a people who need their own tie with those beauties, their own knowledge of and respect for the delicacy of ecosystems.

3.

Never that people are pointless – the people who live here are the Pacific Northwest. The ones we meet form the structure of our lives, just as the outline of the area and its natural beauty form the outline of what we may believe about God.

Who are these people? I do not know them all yet. I am a Scandinavian American and my childhood was more or less blond and pale. My father is a retired pharmacist, but he did not own his drugstore, so he belonged to a union. Of my mother's brothers, one graduated from college. My mother had an education in classical music. Our neighbors were also Indians, but we never thought of ancestral background, we were just friends. Their mother taught school. My father brought home beaded pins shaped like Indian Chiefs, said an Indian woman who made them sold them to him at the drugstore, and my sister and I kept our pins forever. Throughout high school the one black child was an Ethiopian exchange student. De facto segregation may not have seemed strange to an accepting child, but today it seems odd. In college I met many immigrants from other ancestries, people who must have sprung from the slave trades, or indigenous peoples of the area. They are not labeled this way in my photo albums, but they make the world look like that beautiful rainbow we want to be true. There are conflicting interests, lives end, violence and hardships happen, small hardships undermine endurance, but there are those photographs of young people in school.

American poetry and Northwest poetry make my photographs enlarge and expand. The ideal world is many peoples and the poetry world I know is open to everyone. It is the lives of the poets that make me say I want to be myself, whatever that has to be, to write poems from my own life and imagination. The poets I read do this. The human story on the page includes the mind, actions, intentions, responses, and the reach outwards as our civilization moves toward other galaxies. Sometimes I do not see the stars for the streetlights, so I have to imagine them.

The nature of the Northwest gives me identity—I have imprinted the Northwest as a bird does. The people are a structure; we mutually and continually create each others' lives, we keep a national and world community in mind.

4.

I call the house that serves as the Port Townsend office of the press that published *Memory* and *Shelter* "Dragon Gate," always "Dragon Gate." The owner, Gwen Head, tells me I make her sound like a character from a Daphne du Maurier novel. I say it for that reason, because it sounds romantic and I think the house deserves that name.

The proximity of Port Townsend made an invitation to publish with the press when it began in 1979 or '80 very welcome to me. And lately I read that my graduate school, the Iowa City Writers Workshop, grew from a movement toward regionalism—to value Iowa and the Midwest for itself and build a system of belief to neighbor the traditions of the East instead of reflecting them.[3] My first book was published by Ecco Press of New York. I think *Bad Boats* is well-made and Ecco is generous. But I have been glad to feel nearby Dragon Gate—to know I can reach the offices easily in person. I had easy contact with every stage of making *Memory* and *Shelter*. Of course Dragon Gate publishes San Francisco and Arizona poets and others, so my experience may be unique.

Notes

1. Tomas Transtromer, "From An African Diary," in *Friends, You Drank Some Darkness*, chosen and translated by Robert Bly, Beacon Press, 1975, p. 199.

2. Mike Lipske, "Our Long Love Affair with Nature," *National Wildlife*, April-May 1986, p. 43.

3. Stephen Wilbers, *The Iowa Writers' Workshop*, University of Iowa Press, 1980, pp.3-6.

Charles Deemer

Photo by Lloyd M. Dilbeck

CHARLES DEEMER grew up in Virginia, Texas, and Southern California. Educated at U.C.L.A. and the University of Oregon, he has worked as a Russian linguist, a property manager, a college teacher, and an editor. Currently he is full-time playwright-in-residence for Sirius Productions, in Portland, Oregon. Deemer has also written short stories, screenplays, and videoplays. His journalism has appeared in such publications as *The Washington Post*, and *The New Republic*. In 1984, he was awarded the Oregon Arts Foundation Theatre award. His comedy-drama, *Christmas at the Juniper Tavern*, premiered at the New Rose Theatre, and was published in 1985.

Confessions of "An Oregon Playwright"

I've never had a strong sense of place. Born more or less "rootless" into a Navy family for whom travel was frequent and "homes" like Virginia and Texas merely a temporary stop between tours of duty, for whom relatives in the Delaware Valley country of New Jersey and Pennsylvania were people one visited on occasional holidays—I grew up with a crazy mixed-up accent of speech and a sense of keeping my toothbrush ever at the ready.

My accent had been honed along the beaches of Virginia, where I was born in 1939 at the Naval Hospital in Norfolk, and at George Peabody Elementary School in Dallas, where I began school. No doubt the influence of my parents, with their Pennsylvania Dutch roots, was in there somewhere as well. At any rate, by third grade when we were moving yet again, this time to the melting pot of Southern California, my accent was sufficiently foreign, which is to say sufficiently "southern," that my parents were persuaded that I needed Speech Therapy, which the Pasadena School System gave me *gratis* until I spoke like a human being. This isn't the kind of background that gives one a strong sense of place.

I don't recall hearing a thing about the Pacific Northwest by the time I graduated from high school. Indeed, somewhere along the way, in the frequent change of school systems, I had missed the study of geography and to this day cannot identify the states on a U.S. map, despite my travels. But in 1957, having survived the early years of rock-n-roll to graduate from high school and be accepted at Cal. Tech. (where I expected to become a mathematician or an astronomer, to whom a sense of place is, after all, astronomical), I became aware of Oregon, to the north, where my parents planned to settle into early retirement, in Medford.

Since today I have something of a reputation as "an Oregon playwright," at this point it would be properly dramatic to confess that it was love at first sight, that I took readily to the woods and wilds of the Northwest, became a great fisherman and hunter, camped out for weeks at a time, learned to survive on regional flora. In truth, my early memory of Medford was that it was terribly boring. There was no jazz station on the radio. No decent bookstore in town. No one seemed to have heard of Muddy Waters, Little Walter, Howlin' Wolf or any of the other blues artists I was discovering in the late fifties. Medford, and Oregon, must be a fine place to retire since it sure seemed like a boring place to live.

Enjoying the Northwest came later. For reasons too complex to relate here, I dropped out of school in 1959, joined the Army, and became a Russian linguist in the Army Security Agency. In retrospect, it was one of several profound decisions I've made in my life: for three years I received an intense education from my fellow linguists, most of whom were senior to me by five or six years, with Masters Degrees from Berkeley, Yale, Harvard, Chicago and Columbia, graduate students who had joined the Agency ("choice, not chance") a step ahead of the draft. They told me what books to read and became the foundation of an intellectual community I had not been a part of before, not even at Cal. Tech. – and this community, the Army being what it is, had no common geographic roots. Yet one of my senior colleagues, Dick Crooks, was a Northwest fanatic – or to be more precise, a fanatic for the timber and palousse country of northern Idaho.

Dick had nothing if not a sense of place. I was captivated by his deep feeling for "home," and the closer Dick and I became, the more his sense of place became my own. Over German beers and German wine, I could listen for hours to Dick's romantic tales of his northwest Idaho country and its colorful loggers, of drinking and gambling and whoring and carrying-on in towns like Orofino, Pierce, Riggins, Salmon. It was Dick who introduced me to the music of Woody Guthrie (twenty years later I would perform a one-man Guthrie show), particularly to the folk poet's songs about the Columbia River. I heard my first logging jokes from Dick. I learned about something he called "the high lonesome" (later a central image in my short story, "The Idaho Jacket").

After discharge, I visited Dick in Orofino, his home town on the Clearwater River, and with Orofino as home base I was given a guided tour through what suddenly became "God's country," full of raw beauty and raw people. I was finishing up my undergraduate studies at the time, at UCLA, with no notion that I would become a writer. But suddenly, thanks to Dick, I seemed to know where I was. The Pacific Northwest offered dramatic contrast to the buzz and frantic growth of Southern California, which was beginning to wear on me. Perhaps I missed the Atlantic Ocean and

Texas plains of my childhood and longed for wider spaces. Yet I was attracted to the people as much as to landscape: there was something fundamental, genuine and poetic in the manner of the old loggers (some of them Dick's relatives) we uncovered in hideaway homes and bars. I became "a true believer," and years later versions of these same people would begin to populate my plays.

2.

When I began writing fiction in my late twenties, I began with the technical lack of a sense of place, though I didn't realize this at the time. In my short fiction, this was not a serious problem, but in the novel form, to which I began to devote my energy, my inability to create "place" (a fully dimensional environment in which my characters could live) was a major artistic failure. I could create story and character but no sense of atmosphere or environment: the flesh of my people had no skeleton to hang on, and consequently my characters were vague and undefined. It took me no less than three unpublished novels to get the message that I wasn't a novelist. When one doesn't have a sense of place, it's easy to get lost.

In the meantime, while working on an M.F.A. in fiction at the University of Oregon, I began to write plays. My initial motive was greed—a blessing in disguise. The University was offering a fat Shubert Playwriting Fellowship and, like any beginning writer, a contest was justification enough for writing a play. I wrote my first play in competition for the Fellowship and came in second. The next year I won the Shubert, and consequently was required to get my M.F.A. in playwriting, not fiction. But I had taken an immediate liking to playwriting as well: a play didn't take as long to write as a novel (three failed novels had exhausted me); more importantly, in a play one didn't have to create a sense of physical space. The space was the stage itself, and bringing its physical aspects to life was the job of the set designer. Moreover, the flesh of a character was hung on an actor. Here, then, was a form in which my strengths (storytelling and the creation of character) were not hurt by my weakness (not knowing where I am).

In retrospect, I like to think this was an ecstatic moment of discovery, though I cannot pinpoint when it happened. I suppose playwriting just grew on me, like my love of Dick Crooks' Idaho and, by extension, the entire Pacific Northwest—from the hills I wandered east and west of Eugene, to the mountains I visited in Washington and Montana. I graduated with an M.F.A. in playwriting and moved east, surely ready for playwriting's major leagues: I'd eliminated my major technical weakness as a writer with the help of collaborators, Dick and the set designer and the actor. And if alone I didn't have a sufficient sense of place, they gave me one, and together we were going to write some damn good plays.

3.

In early draft the play had the horrible title *Goodbye, America, I Love You*, and it was the first play, story or novel I had ever set out of the west. Most of my work by the mid-seventies was set in Southern California, where I'd spent much of my youth. Typically my work dealt with the confrontation of the city Californian with the rural Northwest, a journey matching my own; but never had I told a story set on the east coast.

Then I wrote a play set on Maryland's Eastern Shore. My usual thematic matter was there, the dramatic confrontation of urban and rural values, but somehow I was shocked to discover that I had actually set a play in the east. "You're becoming one of us," a friend told me. As much as I admired and was fascinated by the watermen of Chesapeake Bay, who had much in common with Northwest loggers, I obviously was an outsider, an observing stranger. Moreover, for the first time in my life I was gaining a rough sense of place; east coast rhythms and density were swift and compact, and I missed the more open and relaxed texture of the west. I returned in 1977, to Portland, Oregon.

Goodbye, America, I Love You became *The Pardon*, the first of a dozen of my plays to premiere in Portland. It is still the only thing I've written set on the east coast.

4.

On the surface, a sense of place has become important in my work in recent years: the Northwest backdrop is thematically important in plays such as *Country Northwestern* (about the last day in a town being flooded by a dam project), *Christmas at the Juniper Tavern* (the comic confrontation of a logging community with an Eastern guru and his followers), *Waitresses* (a mother-daughter story of small town Oregonians with dreams of Nashville). I've named my northwest territory "Juniper County," and although I set Juniper in Central Oregon, there is a considerable influence of Orofino, Idaho, there as well. Each of the plays above has at least one regional joke I first heard from Dick Crooks And I've been lucky to find set designers who create my small town taverns and kitchens with convincing realism. With my collaborators, then, I've succeeded in becoming "an Oregon playwright."

But what does this really mean? After all, I don't always write in regional settings: two of my best plays (in my opinion) have nothing to do with the Northwest – *The Comedian In Spite of Himself* (about the life of Moliere) and *The Sadness of Einstein* (still unproduced as I write, about certain comic possibilities of the new physics). My most successful play, *Christmas at the Juniper Tavern*, draws more from my early 1971 one-act, *The Death of Teng Yen-feng*, than from the Rajneesh phenomenon in Oregon, although I've yet to meet a journalist who believes me when I say this.

In fact, I consider my major playwriting influences to come from the Europeans, with their stronger sense of a theater of ideas, than from the naturalistic Americans. The sense of place in *Our Town*, in which Wilder's dramaturgy cast influences throughout Europe (as Durrenmatt and others have acknowledged), is different from the sense of place in Neil Simon's New York or David Mamet's Chicago, where physical territory can be important. Thorton Wilder wrote of places in the mind, and except for Albee, early Sam Shepard and Arthur Kopit, few of his artistic disciples in the U.S. have gained wide audiences. "The inside of my head is my country," a character of mine sings, and this allegiance is my own.

If this suggests a fragile allegiance to the Northwest, I admit it. The dramatic opposition of things urban and rural, which is so central in my work, can be set in many environments. I have a sense of being "a westerner" but less of being "a Northwesterner." Most of my stories would work in the Southwest, the small communities of Northern California, the Nevada desert, or on a Hawaiian island. I set many of my plays in Oregon because I live here; I like it here, but I claim no special significance for the region, as I make use of it, other than its being a part of "the (vanishing) west."

I'm sure there is a tradition of Northwest literature but I don't feel that I am a significant part of it. That tradition belongs to poets and novelists who grew up here, who hunt and fish (I still don't), who can use a chain saw without endangering life and limb – the kind of people whom I often put in my plays. As "a regional writer" I suppose I'm something of a spy, "stealing" from the direct experience of others, but like it or not, I find myself called "an Oregon playwright" as if this were especially significant. Indeed, recently a critic wrote that *Christmas at the Juniper Tavern* is "an Oregon classic" but I haven't the slightest idea what this means. To me, the play is philosophical comedy (even a Zen comedy) about the comic clash of Western and Eastern values and versions of reality. Its relationship to the Rajneesh phenomenon is accidental but also fortunate in its timing, in that it gave the play a large audience (perhaps for all the wrong reasons). But "an Oregon Classic"?

People have influenced me more than place. Dick Crooks' Northwest became my own but it was probably the magnetism of Dick's personality that made the difference. Portland, which has been very kind to me as a playwright, is kindest with its people. Portland is not an important theatrical town: without an Equity company, it does not belong to the significant regional theater network in this country. To have a play produced in Portland is, frankly, professionally meaningless, as far as one's "resume" is concerned. But Portland is home to Steve Smith, Gary O'Brien, Peter Fornara, Richard Watson and other theater directors and producers who have supported my work for a decade now. They have helped shape my work but this is not the influence of "Portland," it is the influence of living artists who just happen to make Portland their home, as I do.

Perhaps I found these collaborators so readily – and the most important thing about theater is that it is a collaborative art – because Portland is theatrically insignificant in the national perspective: any genuine playwright who happens along readily stands out. Indeed, my agent in New York considers a Portland premiere no premiere at all; Portland doesn't count. But here I am, working away because I like the people I work with here. The "residency" relationships I've had with Portland theater companies is the very best way a playwright can work: I usually have a stage even before I begin to write. And the stage is my canvas, not the white paper that precedes the script. The stage is my canvas, the actors my language, and I've happily found ready access to both in Portland.

There are professional advantages and disadvantages in my situation. I get more work done, and presumably grow more artistically, since I've reduced the anxiety and hassle of "finding a production." At the same time, a Portland production is something of a laboratory test—one can find out much about the strengths and weaknesses of a script, but since Portland is not on the professional theater circuit, there is little communication between Portland and the country's regional theater centers. A play done in Seattle or San Francisco can be seen by directors and producers who matter "in the business" of professional theater. This is unlikely in Portland.

Then why don't I move to Seattle? I ask myself this annually. But interestingly enough, when I think of moving, I usually think of eastern Oregon, or the coast, or even Dick's Idaho country—places where the northwest environment is rural and remote. Perhaps I've come to have a sense of place, after all: a liking for the sound of rivers, wind in the tall trees, the smell of stark desert and white mountain and vast ocean. This place grows on you.

Wherever I am, in Portland or elsewhere, I'll be writing plays set in Juniper County, Oregon, and others that are set elsewhere. I'll continue to set city against countryside, insider against outsider, logger against guru, and (as in a play in progress) folksinger against singing robot. Juniper, I suppose, has become my image of something that is rootedly western, rootedly special, but which is challenged everywhere by new and different values and realities. Space, solitude, individuality, self-reliance—these are the values I associate with the Northwest, as I make use of them as a playwright. But space may be a dinosaur, doomed to disappear, and self-reliance can easily turn into selfishness: these are the parameters of conflict from which drama emerges.

I don't expect to be living in Portland forever. Professionally, I need a larger theater market; I just don't want to have to move there. What one does, I suppose, is hide out to write, and commute into the large cities for production. So I'm rather searching for a place to hide out in these days. Recently, in fact, Dick Crooks and I returned to Orofino, and the Clearwater River looked pretty good. But last year it was Hawaii that looked pretty good. And next year . . .?

In the last analysis, I'm my father's son, always at sea, the Northwest a port that's been good to me but still not quite home. Perhaps the "high lonesome" of Dick Crooks' loggers and the wanderlust of the sailor are related: toothbrush ever at the ready, the human accent mixed-up and crazy, always a step away from needing additional therapy—but who knows where one may find it?

If this is the same thing as being "an Oregon playwright," that's fine by me.

Lawson Fusao Inada

Photo by Christopher Briscoe

LAWSON FUSAO INADA is the author of *Before the War* (Morrow, 1971) – the first book of poetry by an Asian-American to be published by a major firm. As an educational consultant, Inada has conducted numerous workshops, including those for the Modern Language Association, the St. Paul Public School System, and the Iowa State Department of Public Instruction. He has served on the Task Force on Racism and Bias in Education for the National Council of Teachers of English. His poems have been widely anthologized in such volumes as *New Directions 23* and *The United States in Literature*. In 1984 Inada received the Excellence in Teaching Award from the Oregon State Board of Higher Education. Currently he is Professor of English at Southern Oregon State College.

Living in the Northwest

I. A Bit of History

As a Californian (I've lived in Oregon since 1965, but those formative years in Fresno just won't let go; they made me what and how I am), I took the long, slow way to Oregon (you know how real Californians are – they don't consider there to be much of anything north of Sacramento) – from Fresno to the concentration camps and back again, then out to Iowa for some graduate school, and from there to New Hampshire for my first teaching job.

I had started an M.A. at Iowa, but decided to get an M.F.A., and had a nice assistantship waiting for me at U.Mass. Then novelist Tom Williams, my colleague at U.N.H., said, "Why not Oregon?" Oregon? I knew my good Iowa friend, Vern Rutsala, was there, back home, and he had always had good things to say about the place. Then there were Hanson, Hugo, Huff, Kizer, Roethke, Salisbury, Stafford, Wagoner, *Northwest Review*, *Poetry Northwest* – a working tradition. Thank you, Tom!

What to expect? Who knows. The college catalogue had some pictures of forests and mountains, but I had to fill in the rest of the space. At the "gut level," I remembered the huge, soft, white t-shirt one of my uncles had given me to grow into (this was "before the War," as we always say) – it said "OREGON" in bright green letters, with a cartoon of the ol' Oregon Duck. Good memories.

Wham! Ontario at dusk, in the midst of summer. Oregon wasn't any different from Idaho. Then, off in the distance, you could see Burns, but you never got there. McKenzie Pass, that was more like it, and so on into Eugene. I loved the place, still do. Had a very good year – just enough teaching, just enough school, did a lot of writing, put together what became my first book. Made friends I still have. My wife, Janet, was carrying our first child.

Still, when it came time to look for a job, I was thinking of California. But it wasn't thinking of me – so when my only job offer came from a place called Ashland, Southern Oregon College, I jumped at the chance. After all, I'd be hauling in a big 7 grand, a full 2 grand more than I made in New Hampshire. Then, too, we were right on the border, with Fresno being a day's drive away.

In those days, the I-5 freeway wasn't finished, and Ashland, the Rogue Valley, had that sense of isolation. The valley looked good, particularly the very "western" buttes of Table Rock, but it was also a rather remote place. There were two television channels, no bookstores to speak of (the college library took up about a third of one floor of an old classroom building), and the closest good restaurant had to be in San Francisco (I was particularly starved for Chinese and Mexican food, and for the simple things, like soy sauce and tofu). Ashland still had several wigwam burners, several mills going (now there's one, off and on); it was dry, it was hot; it was, well, a lot like California, but.

You've probably heard of Angus Bowmer. He was a college speech teacher; I'd go to meetings with ol' Angus; but in the summers, he'd do his Shakespeare. Then, zoom, things happened – his theater grew (there are now 3 theaters, and the Oregon Shakespearean Festival goes year around). Haight-Ashbury (I remember the first hippie who came to town, a young guy with fairly short hair and a light beard; he got beat up). Vietnam (very little activity locally at first, but after Kent State, the college closed down, and we had a march of several hundred, all the while in touch with "Radio Free Portland"). Communes in the vicinity.

The rest is history. But what all that meant to me, personally, was that the region became, not only much more "livable," but a fundamentally safer place to be. Plain and simple, what with all the actors and tourists and beardeds around, a guy like me wasn't subject to question anymore; I could be an "outsider," a "foreigner," perhaps, but I just might be a spender of money. Plus, at least I wasn't no hippie. And what the heck, I might be from Hawaii (there used to be a sizable group of them on campus). Then, too, I wasn't a Mexican, a Negro, or an Indian (one thing about New Hampshire, it had a big Air Force base, so I could always be "in the military").

Also, there's the rest of history. California was going crazy at the time. I had a couple of kids. I was staying put. I was writing well, publishing, came out with my first book. And on campus, I was doing things – like organizing the few "minority" students we had, recruiting others, setting up and running a program for "ethnic" *and* disadvantaged students (of which there are many in the region), and in the English department, we had a magazine going. But the biggest single historical factor for me was the death of John

Coltrane. And Paul Chambers, Eric Dolphy, Bud Powell, among others. I no longer had a need for cities. Rock was in; jazz was fading away; the clubs went under; even in New York, the bright voices went underground; other musicians moved to Europe.

So I settled into Oregon to stay. Ashland, especially, was developing a lot of "ambience," with California refugees going into business, with people from communes (mostly folks from cities) settling into town and likewise going into business, so now we seem to be a Santa Cruz, a Boulder, that sort of thing. Also, with many migrant workers settling down, we have a bunch of Mexican restaurants, a French restaurant, a Polish restaurant, a Korean restaurant, an Afghanistanian restaurant, a Texas restaurant, health food, stealth food, hazardous food, truck stops, franchise food; we even passed mustard with the Rajneesh, for being strictly kosher.

But what all this means is that we've become "California-ized"—which, to a certain extent, is fine with me. And it also makes natural sense, for this region, despite the border, is very similar to northern California in terms of rainfall, growing season, etc. You can grow palms and eucalypti here; we even have drought. So I'm something of an imposter in this collection, because I'm not a "real Northwesterner." To me, that begins up by Roseburg—and rainfall statistics will bear me out. (And, lest some of you get too heady about your Northwest authenticity, we're all living in the Midwest compared to Alaska—now there's a real place.) Or, according to history, this southern Oregon region came *this close* to becoming the State of Jefferson. So there—we're neither here nor there.

The best of both worlds. California without the madness. The Northwest without the rain. And, since the politicos upstate consistently ignore us or trickle down the dregs, we'll put our money in the Jefferson State Bank (of which there are several branches).

Now, how does this atmosphere affect the lives of our artists? You'd be surprised, for instance, just how many writers there are around here—including those with bonafide "national reputations." People who make a good living at it. But we're an unruly non-group, individuals; we don't hang out together. We work; that's why we're here. Oh, sure, we're friends, colleagues, and sometimes we read together, work together, get together for occasional occasions, but that's about it. No groups, no clubs, no politics, no throats to cut, no backs to stab, no one to exclude, nothing to join, nothing to climb. Just writers writing. Of course, we have our egos, but there's nothing quite like living in the same town with that old poet in the theatrical house to bring you down a notch. Sure, he's only published one book, but . . .

In the meantime, friends stop by, heading somewhere (we're "centrally-located"). Then there's the postal service. The telephone. Sometimes, I'll drive somewhere, or fly (ended up in Europe last year). But I always come back. Why not? There are a lot of hassles out there. You can feel poor out there, out of it (out of what?), inundated (by what?). The way I feel, I don't need it. I've pretty much been there. (One place I particularly respect, which makes sense, considering my features, is the Navajo Nation; the people took me in, and made me feel at home.) So the way I look at it, these surrounding mountains, instead of enforcing isolation, actually function as filters, letting in what matters (though I'd still like to see more foreign films); they also work the other way—you've got to have a reason, no matter how flimsy, to get out.

II. Requirements and Rights

I'm not a "real" fisherman (more like a very occasional "zen" one; but there was the big time when Clint Armstrong, a black Philly chemist living in Medford, and I took a jug of wine and a basket of chicken up into a slow place on the Klamath; we catfished all night, and the next day Clint did those dudes up right, outside on his spread); I'm not a hunter; I'm not even a jogger (in Fresno, it was chasing or fleeing). Or, while I'm at it, I'm not a gardener (my wife is an Oregon State Master Gardener), a skier, a serious cyclist, an actual rafter, or an amateur photographer (what the heck *do* you do, Inada?)—but I require the right to have such possibilities around.

Including sleeping in the back of my crumby pickup. Including filling it up with leaves, or letting the trees fill it up, and then just driving around, scattering, postponing going to our world-class dump (a gorgeous place, actually). Then it gets full of snow, and I'm piloting a glacier. Maybe I will or won't go to a drive-in movie.

I require the raccoon in my yard at night, the owl in the oak, the coyotes yuppie-ing it up in the hills out back. I require the right to stroll out a ways for wild berries (the Takelma had that too, but they're extinct). I require the right to get lost, as I did one time, on the other side of Grizzly Peak (it was a luxury, actually, drinking wild water, blowing my nose on moss, and a porcupine finally showed me the way to a road). I require those trains going up, coming down the Siskiyous (the highest such grade in the nation; the Cascades and Siskiyous meet up at Siskiyou Pass; the Cascades are upstarts, and tend to smile a lot; the Siskiyous mostly frown; I've found seashell fossils up in Siskiyou rocks). I require deer, bear, bobcats around, and I'm sure I'd miss the slugs.

Up past the headwaters of the Rogue, past Crater Lake (which doesn't do much of anything), you can get into the major flyways of the Klamath Basin (or you can keep on going forever—another requirement). They have Vermont-class fall foliage over there. They also grow potatoes, which they store in great ground-covered sheds, which I remember from Quebec (except these folks are Chinese or Czech). That's Klamath and Modoc Country, the home of Edison Chiloquin, "Captain Jack," and our most formidable concentration camp. Grover's Corners it ain't.

I require the presence of Shasta. I've just got to know it's there. You can see Shasta from just north of Sacramento, and you can get a "peak" locally by heading up in that direction. Shasta has a feel, a sound. Shasta is a good reason to be here, or to go to Yreka, for the feel of Shasta. Yreka's one of my favorite towns, because there's always a poem waiting around (say "Yreka Bakery" backwards). And in Hornbrook, there's the "First/Last Chance Tavern"—depending on which way you're going.

I require a good doctor, a good mechanic, and access to Les Schwab (for you non-Northwesterners, ol' Les runs a series of "tire centers"—and tires are an item of conversation, which figures; as a matter of fact, around here, we don't drive cars or trucks, we drive *rigs*). I require access to the ocean (back east, many of the beaches are "private"; on the Oregon coast, I've seen public whales), the redwoods, the desert (where you've got to have good tires); I require access to the Bay Area, to Portland (Powell's Books, Tower Records)—for regular "cultural raids." And, lest we forget, I love the Northwest public libraries—Seattle, Portland, Eugene, Medford, Ashland—where you can go in and relax, like you own the place.

All of this affects my work as a writer. So, okay, I'm a "Northwest writer"—it shows. (The best piece of Northwest writing I've seen is the surrender speech of Chief Joseph.) It's in the landscape, what's around. That's the way I am; I can't help it. Thus, I am also a California writer, a New England writer, a New York writer, a Midwest writer, a Missouri writer, a Southwest writer, and also a European (particularly German) writer. Etcetera. I've written "in" Zimbabwe, too, Alaska, the tropics—whatever the muse and music say.

But sooner or later, living in the Northwest, you've got to write some Chinese poetry, some Japanese poetry—it comes with the territory, the Pacific Rim. Which fits right in with what I always am—an Asian-American writer. And it just so happens that the Northwest is *the* spawning ground of Asian-American literature. Carlos Bulosan, Frank Chin, Mine Okubo, Yoshiko Uchida, Louis Chu, Jeffery Chan, Shawn Wong, Monica Sone, Ed Miyakawa, Ron Takaki, John Okada, Bienvenido Santos, Frank Miyamoto, Takeo Nakano, Toshio Mori, Garrett Hongo, Alan Lau, Laureen Mar, Lonny Kaneko, James Omura, Bill Hosokawa, James Sakamoto, Jesse Hiraoka, James Mitsui, Alex Kuo, Stephen Sumida, Mei-Mei Berssenbrugge, and so forth—these are all Asian-American writers who are from the Northwest, have lived in the Northwest, are living in the Northwest, or are published by the University of Washington Press. We've had generations here, from the early 1800s at least—merchants, farmers, miners, railroad workers, cowboys . . . We came to settle, to stay, to establish a tradition. We've also had to fight, and it is no mere coincidence that the two most famous resisters against the World War II evacuation, Gordon Hirabayashi and Minoru Yasui, are from Seattle and Portland, respectively. We're still in court.

If you're interested in any of this, go down to David Ishii Bookseller, Pioneer Square, Seattle. Or write the University of Washington Press, for a brochure. In the meantime, I think I'll head over to the Yamada spread on the Applegate River. Just to say hello. They've got a ranch, and a bunch of us gather there every year in December, to make mochi, and to keep the Northwest going as it ought to go.

III. Developments, Directions

Now, lest I seem a bit too cozy, too settled, too "Northwesternish," too whatever, I'll go on a bit, time permitting. (I work at a working-class college, I work on several "fronts," which I'll describe, and I also have to work in the summers—but the way I look at it, I've also got something to teach, particularly in the area of so-called "minority" literature and culture. My wife is an elementary teacher; we were in the Iowa Writers Workshop together. We've got college-age sons—one's at Yale, the other will be at Columbia. Life in the Northwest gets expensive.)

The point is, it took me a while to "get situated," but the Northwest has become my "base of operations"—a starting place, "where I'm coming from." Thus, much of my literary work is directed, and takes place, elsewhere—in the greater world. Also, because of various developments, my concept of "literary work" has evolved enormously from when I first started writing. (Among other things, I consider myself to be a "classically-trained" poet. I don't know what else to call it. My main *sensei* at Fresno State was Phil Levine, Jewish/Detroit, who was sentenced to Fresno after having served time at Iowa and Stanford, where he worked with Yvor Winters, who was also Momaday's mentor, among others. As a result, I put in two years at the Levine Conservatory, working in English, American, and international traditions.) Compared to today, there were very few magazines then (my first "real" publication was in the *San Francisco Review*—George Hitchcock, originally from Oregon, in his pre-*Kayak* days), and the opportunities for giving poetry readings were extremely limited (my first "real" reading was with Morton Marcus, who managed to get the popcorn machine turned off in the lobby of the Faris Theater, Palo Alto, while the movie was going on). Poetry wasn't a "thing" yet; plus, there seemed to be two "leagues"—"academic" and "beat."

So much for those distinctions. Now, everybody's a poet (or a guitarist or lyricist), and poetry's an industry—which is fine with me. Because it means audience, including "live" audience. Which fits right in with my pre-literary orientation—jazz music—and which works right in with the ancient muse/music tradition. So, in the vernacular, "I'm ready to blow"—anytime, anyplace, with anyone, including any musicians. A luau, a pow-wow, a bar mitzvah, a Buddhist service—I'm ready, with something new for the occasion. I've worked the New York Public Theater, Madison Square Garden, but the most fun, and challenging, were those gigs with the East-West Players and musicians from the "Hiroshima" group in the public parks of L.A. (including East L.A., where the picnickers didn't necessarily speak English, so I worked out an act with poetry, puppets, and dancers), and the most meaningful were those Japanese-American "Days of Remembrance" in Seattle and Portland, where thousands attended.

Then, too, with the "rise of ethnic awareness," and the concern with the teaching of writing, I get invited here and there. That's what got me to Europe last summer, for the first time (sponsored by the U.S. Information Agency), to participate in West Berlin's "Horizonte '85" (a festival devoted to Asian culture), and to lecture throughout Germany. Very interesting. I was the only Asian-American to participate in the festival, and, not ever having been abroad, I had my eyes opened for me. That is, the German, Japanese, Korean, Swiss, Indonesian, and P.R.C. writers all regarded me in a very new way: "Who is he?" I mean, I could have been batting .300 in the Northwest League, but they couldn't care less. I was some sort of cultural upstart from this huge new country founded by illiterate immigrants. Luckily, as a Fresnan, and Fresno is the most cosmopolitan place I've ever been (many of my childhood friends were "ethnic German"), I was eventually able to "relate"–but then came that dinner with Gunter Grass in attendance.

"Uh, hi, Gunter–my name's Inada; I'm an Asian-American writer and I live in the Northwest." Pause. Then: "So many of you American writers live in ivory towers. What do you know of the world?" Back to my seat. That night I began a poem, which was coming anyway–a little 10-page, jazz haiku ditty called "Rebuilding Berlin." When I got back home, I typed it up and sent it to him (at his "work" address, a museum he supposedly "directs"), with a letter that said something like: "Dear Gunter: I take exception to what you said, because there are no 'ivory towers' here in Northwestern America, and I also know a few things from having experienced war. Enclosed is a poem about your city, and also my very working-class cap." (I hated to part with it, actually, since it said "Les Schwab" and the local franchise dealer gave it to me personally; at the same time, I figured it was, fittingly enough, a gift from the Northwest German-American tradition: "If we can't guarantee it, we won't sell it.") He never answered. But I'm sure he got the message.

At Amerika Haus Berlin, several American writers gave lectures to high school ("gymnasium") teachers, all of whom spoke fluent English and were very well-versed in American studies (more so than many American teachers; and they certainly know more about "us" than we know about "them"). Ishmael Reed, my longtime colleague (Ishmael is the founder of the very important Before Columbus Foundation), was there. My lectures were on Northwest literature (they know about Oregon, since the Rajneesh has large holdings in West Berlin—which perhaps figures), and Asian-American literature (they of course know about "our" camps). Then E.L. Doctorow (who, because of a minor "glitch" in his passport, almost didn't make it through The Wall; the guards, of course, were fully armed, and speaking Russian; compared to Doctorow, I was totally kosher), his wife, and I were treated to a tour of East Berlin—where we went by Brecht's theater and the nearly-adjoining graves of Brecht and Hegel. (Bach's East German home was off-limits, but my wife and I later managed to go through the territories of Heine, Dante, Moliere, etc.)

What does all this mean to a Northwest writer? Well, for some time now, and I write this during the Russian nuclear disaster, I've considered my territory to be internationl: I teach "foreign" work when I can, I've tried my hand at translations, and I've attempted to deliberately write pieces that could somehow "transcend," or at least diminish the difficulties of, translation. Then, too, on a very related "front," my local colleage, David Zaslow (a poet originally from Brooklyn; combined, we become "Zen Judaism"), and I have gone into business, forming a children's media and publishing company called Kids Matter—which is our way of trying to make a difference in the world of education. (Business, or rather, putting out money where my mouth is, is nothing new to me; Jeff Chan, Frank Chin, Shawn Wong, and I put up the funds to publish John Okada's great novel, *No-No Boy*—now published by U.W. Press.)

I am what and where I am, but my relatives fought across Europe and took part in the liberation of Paris; also, there are more "Japanese-Americans" in South America than here; therefore, for me to limit myself to anything less than the world would be ridiculous. After all, it's not simply a matter of "living in the Northwest"—but living, period. And northwest of what?

Madeline DeFrees

Photo by Dan Hillen

MADELINE DEFREES was born in Ontario, Oregon, and moved soon afterward to the western part of the state where she attended parochial and private schools. After being graduated from high school at sixteen, she entered the Sisters of the Holy Names of Jesus and Mary where she was known for many years as Sister Mary Gilbert. In 1973, she received a dispensation from her religious vows. DeFrees has taught at several institutions, including Fort Wright College, the University of Montana, and the University of Massachusetts–Amherst, where she directed the creative writing program. She has received grants from the Guggenheim Foundation and from the National Endowment for the Arts. Currently she lives in Seattle.

Sea-Fever:
The Subjective Geography
of the Poem

And will I go back with the reddening
salmon, escape the long upstream
of traffic, my Nova rusted out,
to a town in full view
of the sea?[1]

If the key to the romantic sensibility is the fluid interchange of subject and object, it follows that the geography of the poem is necessarily subjective.[2] This observation is based on the fact that both perception and memory are highly selective and that the poet perceiving and remembering is affected at the time of writing by both internal and external forces. Chief among them may be the prevailing psychic and emotional currents. Kicking Horse Reservoir is dark from more than "the black blue Mission range" and Phillipsburg looks a little more gray viewed from a long interval since the last good kiss.

Geography is by definition a descriptive science concerned with earth's surfaces; and by etymology, a kind of "earth writing." Poetry, on the other hand, must always move beyond the purely descriptive and the superficial. When we speak of "the geography of the poem" or *The Geography of the Imagination* (Guy Davenport's title), we are already in the realm of metaphor: a "territory" assigned to the poet from Aristotle onward. Such a landscape, seen through the poet's lens, will necessarily be colored by feeling—a quality the poet cultivates as assiduously as the scientist tries to avoid it.

But *sound* may be, often is, even more important than feeling, however arbitrary the ear cultivated by a particular poet. And though there may be smaller margin for deviation in traditional verse, I'd hate to stake my fortune on the premise. It may be that the principles governing taste in free verse are less readily identifiable, with the result that formal verse appears more susceptible of laboratory analysis. As a general rule, the narrower the channel, the deeper the river runs.

> In Xanadu did Kubla Khan
> A stately pleasure dome decree:
> Where Alph, the sacred river, ran
> Through caverns measureless to man
> Down to a sunless sea.[3]

In Coleridge's poem, the gardens that follow, the walls and towers, the greenery, may suggest England but only in the most general way. Certainly, the sunny pleasure dome with its caverns of ice seems out of place on the Thames, and the damsel with the dulcimer is assigned to Abyssinia precisely to endow her with a non-English opulence. As Coleridge himself tells us in the poem, we are looking at "a dome in air," and the reader will instantly recognize the honey-dew and milk-of-Paradise diet that sustain the poet.

If my choice of poem seems unfair and outmoded, skip forward a couple of centuries to William Stafford's "Lake Chelan":

> They call it regional, this relevance—
> the deepest place we have: in this pool forms
> the model of our land, a lonely one,
> responsive to the wind. Everything we own
> has brought us here: from here we speak.[4]

Since Northwest readers, at least, know that Lake Chelan is an actual place, the question is: What is the *here* from which the poet claims to speak for all of us? How does the lake in the poem differ from the actual lake? In other terms, what does the poem give us that the travel folders don't? How does the vicarious experience of the poem extend geography? These are questions that distinguish between the lake on the map, the lake in the hills, and the lake in the language, much as a painting may be differentiated from its subject.

At this point it may be helpful to introduce a brief glossary:

sense of place: correspondence between a person's physical and imaginative locale

alien: one whose physical and psychic space fail to correspond; a displaced person *here*: the area in which one is; the immediate physical environment

there: an environment distant in time or space, which, by contrast, confirms the existence of a here[5]

anywhere: a "place" imperfectly apprehended; a synonym for nowhere

somewhere: a paradoxical "place" with vague limits; the opposite of everywhere; a starting point

everywhere: the "place" favored by the upwardly mobile; the habitation of the godlike; realm of omnipresence

bi-location: the ability to be in two places at a time, either as a means of escape or to enjoy the delight of an elsewhere; sometimes called fantasy or out-of-the-body travel

elsewhere: a place which attracts by real or illusory merits not perceived in the here

indigenous: having originated in and being produced, growing, living, or occurring naturally in a particular region or environment; native

subjective geography: a way of relating to place that allows one to enjoy its advantages without suffering its negative effects. This need not preclude representing the place in negative terms

These definitions are only partly facetious. If their function is to clarify discourse for the writer, it follows that the reader will share in the dividends. Meanwhile, it may be useful to inquire into the function of place for the poem and for the poet. Such an inquiry should serve to define indirectly some of the differences between scientist and poet, geography and poetry.

One function of place in the poem may be to create a context for the meeting of reader and writer. This may be far more complicated than it sounds because the variables in the situation approach infinity. The properties of language, especially in poems; the nature of perception; the fitful character of attention; and the subjective biasses of both writer and reader: all these are such that the real miracle occurs when poet and reader meet in a "place" familiar enough to both to extend the reader's awareness as any good poem ought to do. To illustrate some of the possibilities, consider the hypothethical cases of Poets A, B, and C with respect to Readers X, Y, and Z.

Poet A's poem titled "Somewhere, U. S. A.," snags the attention of Reader X as she flips through a magazine over mid-morning coffee. Piqued by seeing the name of her home-town over a poem—one of those extra-terrestrial experiences remembered through the haze of youthful Mr. Shelley's high school English class, Reader X actually peruses the poem, word by word. But Reader X is an alien in Somewhere, in spite of the fact that she has lived there for 42 years, so she writes an angry letter to the Somewhere *Clarion*, taking Poet A to task for his failure to understand Somewhere, his inability to represent the town, and his general inferiority to Keats and Kilmer.

Poet A reads the letter and fires off a retort, which in due course, is also published in the *Clarion*. I have before me just such a letter. It is headlined, "Not about Dixon" and signed "Richard Hugo." In the letter, Hugo insists that "For Schmauch's edification, poems are works of imagination and are not intended to be factual accounts." He goes on to say, "I love Dixon as I love all places that trigger my imagination and lead me to truth about the human condition that I can reveal." Hugo warms to his subject as he writes:

> Schmauch's claim that all people who don't live in Dixon wish they did is nonsense and unless she is bananas she knows it. I love Dixon because a lot of people would not want to live there and many would not even notice it in any detail as they drove through. If Schmauch has to delude herself this way to work up any enthusiasm for a place as unique as Dixon, then her real feelings for the place must be thin indeed.

After a few more sentences in this vein, Hugo concludes:

> Schmauch's chamber of commerce platitudes only cheapen what Dixon really is. We often fool ourselves about the value of an acquaintance, never about the value of an enduring paramour.

Readers of *The Triggering Town* will be familiar with Hugo's idea that the town is merely the generating subject, as opposed to the real subject. They may also recall his belief that it is necessary to "own" a place in order to write about it, and that the odds favor neglected places over the famous tourist attractions "owned" by everyone.

In these matters, the presumption is not always on the poet's side. Consider a second imaginary case. Poet B is given to writing "tourist poems" as in Sandra McPherson's, "I hate tourist poems." Poet B confronts every new experience as if it were an Andalusian bull he must grab by the horns and wrestle to the ground. When Reader Y keeps her appointment with Poet B in Somewhere, U. S. A., while he is off in Anywhere, hundreds of miles distant, the poet is to blame for the failed connection.

Finally, lest we be accused of unrelieved pessimism, let us suppose a happier conjunction. Poet C, who happens to live Here, is so struck by a brief visit to There, that he goes home and writes a poem, which he publishes under the title, "What Happened Over There." The events of the poem are purely imaginary, but Reader Z soon recognizes that they are better than actual. *This* poet sees beneath the surface features (the geography) of There to the human dimension, which is universal. Without overlooking the distinctive qualities of the place, the poet identifies the timeless elements, and Reader Z is so impressed that he puts a copy of the poem over his desk at the waterworks. After that, he keeps fat poets in slim volumes in the top left desk drawer at work and on the nightstand at home. Six months later, Reader Z gives up his job to enter the creative writing program at the University of Somewhere, Poet C's campus. Corny, yes. But poetry, like contemplation not primarily political, may lead—and often does—to significant action. Chances are, when Reader Z completes the degree, he'll be out of a paying job, but he'll be hooked on writing and resourceful enough to support his habit.

Everything we own/ has brought us here. I'm tempted to say that the main reason for my persistent alienation was that I spent more than three decades not owning anything. It's an in-joke with a grain of truth, and to dramatize it, I could say that I spent the first 16 years of my life under the dining room table with a dustcloth while my mother's talk-show went on non-stop. The next 30 or so, I learned to "fret not at [my] convent's narrow room," which was not a room of one's own, but, they said, vastly better. In Montreal and New York, in Oakland, Portland and Seattle; in Durban and Nagasaki, a Sister of the Holy Names could find a convent of her congregation, a home. But for the person whose place is the "not here," such extensive real estate merely reinforces the feeling of estrangement. As Hugo once said when, citing Wordsworth, I

119

reminded him that one didn't have to be *in* a particular place while writing the poem: "Yeah, that's right. But you've gotta be *somewhere*. Because, Buddy, if you ain't *somewhere*, you're not goin' *no place*."

2.

> I must down to the seas again, to the lonely sea and the sky,
> And all I ask is a tall ship and a star to steer her by,
> And the wheel's kick and the wind's song and the white sail's shaking,
> And a grey mist on the sea's face and a grey dawn breaking.[6]

"I think Andy had a ship on his shoulder." My Swedish landlady hoisted a large box to the dumpster, turned it upside down, and released a cascade of mud-encrusted boots, reeling cassettes, and rusty kitchen tools. Notwithstanding her diminutive size, Vivi Ann was a ferocious worker.

"You can put the lid down." She called me from the trance in which I was watching Andy struggle to shift the schooner to the opposite shoulder. His long chestnut hair tangled dangerously with the rigging. Just as I was about to go on to potato ships, poker ships, blue ships, until all the ships were down, a voice intruded, louder this time: *I'm finished. You can let go.*

"Well, I'm relieved," I said, returning abruptly to the here and now. "I won't have to put up with Disco at two a.m. Not to mention the Hammond organ. I tried phoning Andy, the way you told me, but it never helped for more than twenty minutes." Secretly, I had come to believe that Andy was a ship off the old block, incapable of conversion, just as I was unable to relinquish my obsession with the sea.

Like Andy, I had a ship on my shoulder ever since my first and only boat trip—five hours from Portland to Astoria—on one of the old sternwheelers, the *Georgiana*. Born under the sign of Scorpio, I considered water my element, and after the first glimpse of ocean, the western edge became my territory. Although my home-town, Hillsboro, is only a couple of hours from the beach, we didn't own a car, so we seldom went to the coast except with my cousins, and then infrequently. Nevertheless I staked my claim to the lonely sea and the sky . . . the grey dawn breaking, appropriating even the English spelling. (Hugo's *gray* was American; mine was British, a single vowel signalling the status of the alien—that is, *belonging to another person, place, or family; strange, foreign, not of one's own.*) The grey mist and the grey dawn were focal points, not the tall ship and the star. I was letting go of illusion.

I see that we're headed into the treacherous waters of memory. Not far ahead lies Deception Pass. Is there a reliable map? I must turn the question back on the asker. I have already subscribed to the notion that geography may be largely subjective. As for autobiography, with Claude Simon I believe that it is "the most fictitious of forms."

I'm beginning to feel like Noah. I've constructed this cumbersome seaborne craft miles away from the ocean. Landlocked in Montana with Richard Hugo, I can't figure out how to launch it. I might say that I was drawn to dangerous waters because my mother was afraid of them. That the moon was a major influence on my biological tides:

> Pale driftwood demons haunt my shifting coast
> cold in the lunar light, as bones outspread
> on windy beaches where the reaching wave
> wakes tidal terror in the driven blood.[7]

I could talk about learning to swim, feel again the tension and exhilaration of trying to stay afloat in the heated Seaside Natatorium before testing my strength against the ocean. When I consider the buoyancy of my nerve, I return to the enormous effort in that steamy, debilitating concrete tub, arms flailing, breath held, eyes squinched shut against the chlorine: my refusal to give up. And later, the shock of the cold brine, astringent tightening of skin, the excitement of being pummelled by the waves, the taste of salt, sputter and cough of an ocean taken in. The slight heart murmur my doctor detected on my next visit was proof that I had made Pacific rhythms my own.

> Hollow with the tug and slap
> of far tides in a strict cove, I swallow
> the whole ocean at one look
> and in the shadow of the rock, breathe
> in the drift of the sand.[8]

The sea represented freedom, escape, beauty romantically intensified by danger.

> Currents diverge where distance calls,
> pull at the weight, recoil and spring,
> draw like a draught, sink back, subside,
> ride in a blue world lower than light.
>
> Bound to no shore, I sheer and tack,
> veer in the wake of wreckage flung
> at steady stars in a reeling sky;
> then old as earth
> unaltered in my round,
> swing in the compass of the undertow.[9]

Destruction, as Maritain reminds us, is the obverse of creation. A fragment floats up from the past. Conrad, I think. "In the destructive element, immerse . . ." Or is it *alien* element? And is it really Conrad? What is certain, I felt drawn to that destructive element and from my first visit on, began to spend much of my time "Off the Coast of Council Bluffs":

> I studied
> the map of my head, painted the hull
> orange. The mainsail was blue
> over musical water . . .[10]

The task of constructing a family history from my mother's orphan past and my father's reticence left me free to choose my own materials. The distance, the wreckage, the blue world lower than light were indigenous and I appropriated them for my purposes, the long perspective of geology allowing me considerably more leeway to accommodate geography.

The authority of the language is the warrant for the credibility of autogeography. "Is it true?" you ask, and I'm inclined to say I don't know, except that Hugo cured me of saying that. When I showed him an early draft of "Driving Home," ending: "I think/ one more time/ of your black luggage on my bed. I do not know/ if it will carry me much longer," Hugo frowned, the map of his forehead thrown into instant relief. "Don't say, 'I don't know,'" he said. "Say, '*I know it may not* carry me . . .'" Some 15 years later, the Ghost of Overstance at my left shoulder, I *know* that the sea must have been in my poems from the beginning.

When I was in the seventh grade, my teacher assigned a Mother's Day poem, the first I remember writing. It begins: "That mother who has guided me/ through the depths of *life's great sea* . . ." The lines go on in this dogged doggerel way to four or five stanzas considered a triumph for an 11-year-old. What interests me now, beyond the sheer badness of the verse and the tired metaphor, which seems to emanate from an octogenarian, is the curious lack of focus. The grandiose public stance of the opening lines is a way of distancing the mother in time and space, partly by putting her in third person and the relationship in present-perfect tense, an action completed in the past. At the end of each stanza, a refrain shifts to second person, present tense, in the best manner of greeting card verse: "I love you, Mother dear!" It is as if the ritual pieties can only be sustained in this exclamatory way by absenting the speaker.

And that is, indeed, the way I remember it. I had already learned the art of bi-location which was to serve my purposes during long years in the convent when I was often required to be the "companion" to another Sister on a shopping trip or a visit to the dentist. I simply switched to Automatic Pilot and worked on my poems, developing the capacity to carry stanzas in my head, even revise them, without losing track until my first opportunity to write them down. My "notebook" was usually the back of an envelope from a recent letter, carried in voluminous pockets, along with pen and pencil. If we were allowed to speak at supper that evening, the superior might ask whether we had passed a particular building, and when I had to say I didn't know, I was sometimes reprimanded for not paying attention, even though I could as easily have been commended for observing "custody of the eyes." Whether or not the *here* is illusory, as some early philosophers have argued, mine often was:

> Moored to my own
> tilted deck, I ride, I am riding
> the battered hulk to the ocean floor.[11]

During the strict canonical year following the first six months of the Holy Names novitiate, we were allowed to study only theology and philosophy, and our reading was severely restricted. I found my matter in the poems of Gerard Manley Hopkins, "The Wreck of the Deutschland" an immediate favorite:

> I am soft sift
> In an hourglass—at the wall

> Fast, but mined with a motion, a drift,
> And it crowds and it combs to the fall;
> I steady as a water in a well, to a poise, to a pane . . .[12]

The quality of my reading was improving. The preoccupation with water, an element Teresa of Avila considered an aid to mental prayer, continued. Beyond that, the passage just quoted combines passive and active in interesting ways: "I am . . . mined," "I *steady* . . ." The speaker is aware of being acted upon, something the past participle emphasizes, but there is also some sense of independent action carried by the finite verb, along with the curious choice of the indefinite article before *water*.

These two aspects of writing—the active effort and the passive (or better, *receptive*) waiting—in their extreme forms, frenzy and paralysis—are part of the romantic sensibility. The times without water—the dry times—are largely endurance contests, a reaching of the roots towards the saving element.

The ideal geography of the poem may even be a negative geography analogous to Keats's negative capability in the personal order. For such an ideal, a measure of silence is essential, along with a certain solitude. Best of all, the single figure—or two sharing a solitude—against a backdrop of sky and mountain. Barring that, the anonymity of the stranger in a crowd who feels a space around her and a distance. The attempt to bridge the distance evokes the poem, a word from the deepest voice we have. Such utterance makes the place both relative and relevant. Water, with its power to mirror and distort, gives back and takes in. Transparent or opaque, it is the perfect medium. Set the water in motion, and the possibilities are unlimited. Transcending geophysical barriers, the poet returns on the magic carpet of his verse. Consider, for example, this passage from Yeats's *Autobiography*:

> . . . I had still the ambition, formed in Sligo in my teens, of living in imitation of Thoreau on Innisfree, a little island in Lough Gill, and when walking through Fleet Street very homesick I heard a little tinkle of water and saw a fountain in a shop-window which balanced a little ball upon its jet, and began to remember lake water. From the sudden remembrance came my poem "Innisfree," my first lyric with anything in its rhythm of my own music.[13]

At this point, let me anticipate an objection: the mountains in my ideal geography should pose no problem for the mid-westerner or the desert dweller. A healthy poetic faith will move them instantly if that is required, but for me, they are essential, second only to the sea.

Given the psychic distance of Fleet Street and the little tinkle of water, helped along by the oceanic feeling, the poet builds a bridge in air to his own music. The shop-window, the "here" the poet speaks from is little more than a pretext. The text itself is the poem, and, regardless of the physical setting, the poet is no longer at sea but at home in the world.

Notes

1. From "New England Interlude," *Magpie on the Gallows*, by Madeline DeFrees, Port Townsend: Copper Canyon Press, 1982.

2. My thanks to Lois Welch of the University of Montana for allowing me to use her term, "subjective geography."

3. From "Kubla Khan," by Samuel Taylor Coleridge, as reprinted in *The Norton Anthology of Poetry*, Arthur Eastman, et al, Editors, New York: W.W. Norton & Co., Inc., 1970.

4. From "Lake Chelan," *Stories That Could Be True*, by William Stafford, New York: Harper & Row, 1977.

5. See George W.S. Trow, "Annals of Discourse: Forestry," *The New Yorker*, issue of June 11, 1984.

6. From "Sea Fever," by John Masefield, as reprinted in *Familiar Quotations*, John Bartlett, Editor, Boston: Little Brown & Co., 1980. Searching my library for an anthology with Masefield's poem, I was reminded how ephemeral were my early enthusiasms.

7. From "The Undertow," *From the Darkroom*, by Sister Mary Gilbert, New York: Bobbs-Merrill, 1964. This book has long been out of print.

8. From "Barometer," *When Sky Lets Go*, by Madeline DeFrees, New York: George Braziller, 1978.

9. From "The Undertow," *From the Darkroom*.

10. From "Imaginary Ancestors: On My Father's Side," *Magpie on the Gallows*.

11. From "Imaginary Ancestors: Sister Maria Celeste . . .," *Magpie on the Gallows*.

12. From "The Wreck of the Deutschland," by Gerard Manley Hopkins, as reprinted in *The Poems of Gerard Manley Hopkins*, W. H. Gardner and N. H. MacKenzie, Editors, Fourth Edition, London: Oxford University Press, 1970.

13. From *The Autobiography of William Butler Yeats*. New York: Macmillan, Collier Books, 1965.

Sam Hamill

Photo by Paul Boyer

SAM HAMILL was born in 1942, and spent the war years in an orphanage in Ogden, Utah. While serving in the U.S. Marine Corps, he became a conscientious objector. He has studied Zen Buddhism, Taoism, and Confucianism, and spent several years in the Orient. He also attended Los Angeles Valley College, and the University of California at Santa Barbara. In 1972 he and Tree Swenson founded Copper Canyon Press. A printer, editor, writer and scholar widely read in many disciplines, Hamill has published numerous books of poetry, translations, and essays. He has lectured extensively, and worked in Poetry-in-the-Schools programs in eight western states. Hamill has been awarded fellowships from the National Endowment for the Arts, and from the Guggenheim Foundation.

Here and Now

Just three years from now (Spring, 1989), we will note the 300th anniversary of Matsuo Basho's nine-month, 1500 mile walking tour of northern and western Japan. The journal of that journey, the *Oku-no-hosomichi* (*Back Roads to Far Towns* in Cid Corman's translation), is one of the most distinguished and enduring books of these past three centuries, and the most endearing of Basho's diaries.

Basho was a wanderer. His curiosity was at once modest and boundless, his ability to present the universal in a single detail unparalleled. He visited villages and mountain temples and walked the isolated trails with his protege Sora, noting the plants and birds and weather patterns, and observing rites. He was a wanderer who roamed a Japan that never really existed, a Japan that is born today, even in translation, as it was there born in the beautiful slow dance of his brush three hundred years away: a spirit world that is the opposite of the material world we live in.

But it is January, Nineteen-hundred-and-eighty-six. And this is North America. And the only thing that has exceeded the growth of human suffering which accompanies the over-population of the earth is our insane obsession with multiplying our capacity to deliver death. I live just forty minutes by car from one of the most hideous products of mankind—the Trident nuclear submarine base at Bangor.

When I'm troubled, I like to take a short walk out a dirt road from my house, winding down through an old clear-cut and out to a point on a bluff which looks out the Strait of Juan de Fuca. I first walked that road twelve years ago. The clear-cut then was mostly dirt clods and cat-tracks, a few scarred remnants of salal, here and there a blackberry vine or a few mangled spines of fern. It's dense now with life. The alders form a natural canopy. Everything is green.

I watch the fishing boats and shipping lanes. Sometimes I see a submarine and know it is all that is evil in men. At the point where I sit on my stump, there is a tall black lightning-struck ruin of a tree where an eagle nests every summer. Benjamin Franklin thought the eagle a ridiculous symbol for a nation. He much preferred the wild turkey. Now both approach extinction.

A thousand years before Basho's last attack of wanderlust, a middle-aged Chinese gentleman named Tu Fu began a journey of several years' exile from the city, living in abject poverty in thatched huts in the mountains. While the An Lu-shan Rebellion raged, he wrote some of the most humane poetry in the world. And the spirit of his enormous humanity lies in his ability to permit a place to speak through him, always with a long note of compassion:

> Moon, Rain, Riverbank
>
> Rain roared through, and now the autumn night is clear.
> The water wears a patina of gold
> and carries a bright jade star.
> Heavenly River runs clear and pure, as gently as before.
>
> Sunset buries the mountains in shadow.
> A mirror floats in the deep green void,
> its light reflecting the cold, wet dusk,
> dew glistening, freezing on the flowers.

The "place" of the poem is unimportant. It doesn't exist as a reference. The poem is its own place in the same way in which a poem is its own occasion. This could be any river in any green mountain range in any rainy season in the world. Its particularities arise out of the increasingly focused attention to details, moving, line-by-line, to a sharper attention to smaller detail until, in the last line, the "truth of the experience" is realized. And suddenly we understand that what we are seeing, we are seeing only in mirror-image. That the material world we live in is no more or less real than that same world turned upside down in a mirror of water. That being "awake" is a dream.

Was that Chuang Tzu lifting his chalk-white wings from a blossoming scotchbroom that afternoon in August? Can a butterfly become a man in its dreams?

Perched on my favorite stump, I look out at Protection Island, and beyond – the huge empty ocean and blank sky. I listen to the gulls and ravens all year, to summer birds and winter birds, to nighthawks and early morning finches, to birds that mourn, and to birds that celebrate. And I think about how a few small drops of dew freezing on a few dying blossoms over a thousand years ago still speak.

I am a poet in the U.S.A. and I made a conscious choice to live in the shadow economy of my nation—that is, "shadow work" in Ivan Illich's sense of work performed without thought of remuneration for such work—in a specific location, in a particular fashion. As a poet, I am interested only in poetry that is aware of the need to radically alter the policies and priorities of those who rule. I am not interested in the poetry of wit or in pseudo-nature poetry that insists upon personification. It is disheartening to observe on a daily basis the degradation of a singularly materialistic culture. It is sad to know that so many lives pass silently by without having ever glimpsed another world.

But to participate in the continuity of humanity is to remain bound not only to a sense of "place" (whether as a wanderer or as a resident), but to the "other world" as well. Tu Fu is greater than Ronald Reagan because he finds justice—the "other" justice—in freezing dew. He finds it in everyday detail, in natural convergence and daily and seasonal cycles. The "poetic" justice of Tu can save us from ourselves. The "justice" of Ronald Reagan may well kill us all, but it can never *save* a single one of us.

* * *

Basho, happy to be wandering again, came to a temple at Pine Mountain Point, and wrote, "Everywhere between pines graves, bringing home the fact that even vows of 'wing and wing, branch and branch, forever merging' must also come to such, sadness increasing, and at Shiogama Beach a bell sounded evening."

There is nothing to save.

Here, alone on my stump taking notes in the falling mist of the new year, I look far into the west, remembering far east. Basho concluded his journey at Kyoto; in many ways, mine began there.

Hours of sitting, aching back, trying to get my spine straight. Sometimes I thought my knees would break. I struggled with my first few words of Japanese, drank tea, and ate white rice. It was all a dream, but it was beautiful in its time.

Here, a few miles from Port Townsend Bay, I built a house of cedar and fir. The years between were ten years of wandering: from school to school, mountain range to mountain range, river to river. The journals from those years I burned—no use to anyone (except their negative capability), even me. But without those years of wandering, who would I be? What I wrote was not good writing. For all my years of struggle to gain facility with language, all my thinking was unclear.

It seems, looking back over twenty years, like someone else's life, like a long foreign film I somehow got swept up in.

The Zen hermit-monk Ryokan (1758-1831), late in his sixties, met and fell in love with a nun less than half his own age.

> I wondered and wondered
> just when she would come.
> Now we are together.
> What need have I for thinking?

I suppose Ryokan's love poem expresses most of what I feel about this life in this place. With enormous uncertainty, and through all the trials and tribulations imposed by poverty and frustration, I built a small house, most of it alone, but with the generous help of friends as well. I knew somehow that the *doing* of it mattered. I thought about how good it would be never to have to face a landlord or a monthly interest payment, and about how that economic freedom would translate into hours of studytime.

The average U.S. citizen of the male persuasion spends about 5000 minutes per year looking at his own face in the mirror while scraping the hair from his face. I spend about 7000 minutes per year sitting and breathing and leaving things alone. As a nation, we spend almost twice as much money per year on women's hairdos as on medical research.

Building the house, buying it board by board, spending weeks in motels while visiting public schools and prisons to pay for those boards, I thought about very practical matters such as shaving or getting a hairdo, and what those things mean at their most basic level. It is one thing to value a hairdo over medical research. It is quite another not to be aware of having made that choice.

There is almost no astonishment in Ryokan's poem. An old man, he comes to a love he believed in all along, indeed a love he long anticipated. And, having found it at last, finds perfect ease. Although he "wondered and wondered" when or whether he would find it, he did not seek it. He must have wanted it, but he did not wish to be ruled by desire.

And now they are together. He does not wish to possess her, not to be himself possessed by her. He was himself, Ryokan. She was

Teishin. They were together for time and it was good.

The land I paid for, the lumber I bought and nailed . . . this land is not mine. This house my partner suffered and sacrificed to see through to completion . . . while it is "our house" and in the legal sense our land, it is ridiculous to say "I own this land." What passes for love is often pathetic, our claims for things most often enervating and degrading. Another Zen poet, Ikkyu (1394-1481), put it this way:

> What is it in the heart?
> The sound of a pine breeze
> there in the painting.

And Dogen spoke of "enlightenment in the voice of bamboo, heart-radiance in the peach blossom." The Chinese painter Chin Nung said that if one paints the branch well, one hears the sound of the wind.

It is easy to be good; it is impossible to love the devil. We know what is right, but we are not often brave enough to ask ourselves that question, not, at least, at its most basic and meaningful level. The one who listens to a wind in the trees hears a thunderous silence between breezes. There is no truth in words. But when words are used with care, truth may be glimpsed through their framing. Just as the Japanese term *mono no aware* refers to the poignant temporality in the beauty of things. The words are only a pointer. To one who has turned away from death, to one who refuses to see death (as to see life also) in the face (or spirit) of things, the words are almost useless. To the modern Japanese writer Ryunosuke Akutagawa (1892-1927) as he contemplated suicide, it meant that nature would appear to him "more beautiful than it has ever been before."

No potential suicide, I am nonetheless astonished each day to find another day. I work each day at perfecting a kind of heretical Zen discipline. All Zen discipline is heretical. I do not ask myself what certain Zenbos would say about my practice. "If you meet the Bodhidharma, kill him!" Confucius says it this way (in *Chuang Tzu* translated by Burton Watson): "Not to know, not to be able to do—from these things mankind can never escape. And yet there are those who struggle to escape from the inescapable—can you help but pity them? Perfect speech is the abandonment of speech;

perfect action is the abandonment of action. To be limited to understanding only what is understood – this is shallow indeed."

* * *

> Lightning!
> From the darkness, passing,
> the night heron's cry.

Basho wrote this poem perhaps a month before his death. I cannot remember this poem without thinking of the great blue herons that used to nest in Kah Tai Lagoon where we now have a Safeway "superstore" that gives us "everything we want and a little bit more."

Basho's words are not as simple as they at first appear. Robert Aitken, in his excellent study of Basho (*A Zen Wave*), points out how Basho used a Chinese character (*goi*) in naming the night heron rather than the more common Japanese phonetic, *kana*. By making use of the Chinese character, Basho draws an allusion to the five degrees of interfusion of the universal with the particular. Basho's apparent simplicity is, upon closer inspection, an expression of deepest experience.

I do not want to live in a world in which I cannot hear the heron cry. Aitken translates another of Basho's poems:

> How noble –
> The one who is not enlightened
> At a flash of lightning!

Another way to understand this poem is to see it through the following observation of Confucius (again via Burton Watson's *Chuang Tzu*): "When you're betting for tiles in an archery contest, you shoot with skill. When you're betting for fancy belt buckles, you worry about your aim. And when you're betting for real gold, you're a nervous wreck. Your skill is the same in all three cases – but because one prize means more to you than another, you let outside considerations weigh on your mind. He who looks too hard at the outside gets clumsy on the inside."

The one waiting for the lightning flash may never hear the thunder in the silence.

Another old Zenbo I've lived with for many years is the Rinzai monk Hakuin. A contemporary of Thomas Jefferson, he used to go to the Soto meditation halls and poke the other monks as they sat in zazen. "Get up!" he would tell them, "and go do something useful. The work is part of the koan."

For me, the work has most often *been* the koan. I interrupt that work at times to go out into America and poke a few sleepers to see whether they (or I) can be awakened. It would be easy to spend a life in cloisters. It would be easy to practice inaction, especially here where the trees meet the sea and the winds and clouds all sing. But, to quote Ryokan once again, "When I consider the sadness of the world's people,/ Their sadness is mine."

* * *

The best response I can make to the arrogant, banal evil of the Trident nuclear submarine base lies in the simple gesture of nailing one board to another, then adding another, and then another. The hours pile up, the sun and moon slide by, the days grow into weeks and then the weeks into months, and I am still amazed to find that we remain, against all odds, alive.

Looking east, I see the sun high over the Cascade Range. Beyond the mountains, the huge noisy sprawl of the United States. In the past decade, thirty thousand women have died in the U.S.A. at the hands of their "lovers." We will not build them a monument of the sort we built to honor the fifty thousand men we sent to die in Vietnam. We do not "value" their deaths as we define, as a nation, that which is heroic. We say we are an honorable nation where human life is respected. We say everyone gets a vote. We place our faith in a Great American Dream in which we can truly believe. And then we construct an Auschwitz, a Treblinka, a final solution. And if even the mention of an Auschwitz sounds like hyperbole, one must remember that we shall send our Auschwitz out over the world where it will kill not only soldiers, not only Jews or Blacks or Latinos or less-than-human things like Communists, but where it will incinerate every living thing.

We have written our history in blood. And unless we understand how that came to be, we shall write our future in human suffering as well. The government of the United States of America broke *each* of the first 389 treaties it signed with Native American nations. Is this land where I sit making notes for an essay not their land? And will it not become the land of future generations if we manage, somehow, not to bring on armageddon? Don't we belong to the land?

We cannot lie about the land the way we lie and pretend to ethics. Land is neither good nor bad, but is land. In the course of a decent life, the land yields sustenance, a livelihood, and feeds also the spirit by yielding a sense of place, of order, and layers of mythology—a personal mythology, a family mythology, then that of community, etc.—which keep us in touch with ourselves, with one another, and with the continuities of history.

The Navajo have a custom by which one gives away something of one's own to another with whom one has just become friends. The gift is accompanied by a semi-public declaration of friendship. The first time I witnessed it, I was slightly uncomfortable throughout. I was relieved I wasn't the recipient. Over many years, it kept creeping back into my mind—I was a boy watching a man take off his bracelet and give it to another man and speak a kind of vow. When I was small I wondered whether it was like getting married. It wasn't until many years later that I realized that what embarrassed me so was the fact that I didn't have any real friend.

Making a peaceful world begins in making peace with one's self. Since the self is not detached from one's environment, one must make peace with the environment as well. Husbandry and wyfdom speak of land and sea, of proper care and the self's sense of proportion, of silence and of "making waves." Love that is founded on the notion of possessiveness and exclusivity is not love. The poem which objectifies one's lover is not a love poem. We cannot evade responsibility for the deaths we permit each day by pretending the victims are other than ordinary people who are most often born hungry and suffer all their lives and die. We cannot "save life" by serving as merchants of death any more than we can contribute to love by objectifying our lovers.

* * *

If there is a hope for our culture, if we are to avoid self-annihilation, that hope lies in self-discipline, in cultivation, and in rejuvenation. To make the world young again (re-juvenation), it must become more feminized, for the most "feminine" attributes are those we most desperately need: fluidity and interior abundance and communion, all in direct opposition to masculine rigidity and possessiveness and violence. And if honor and dignity and responsibility do not begin in the self, in the home, in the community, where will they begin?

One searches for a balance between the receptive and the responsive. These attributes apply to everything from the use of language to loveplay, from right work to proper inactivity, from economics to philosophy.

Because I was among the last of the generations born before The Bomb, I am among the last to have enjoyed a childhood that entertained a belief in "the future." But public education soon brought me (and all subsequent generations) face-to-face with the realities of a world in which "technological achievements" lead directly into final and irrefutable disaster, and in which even the vehicle of "higher learning" itself, the university, has, to paraphrase Sen. William Fulbright, betrayed a sacred public trust by becoming dependent upon government-subsidized research and thereby becoming no more than employment agencies for the technocracy of death.

One must therefore, if one is to live life without killing, live in the shadow economies of industrialized nations, avoiding even traditional "Marxist" tactics as defined in the Sixties by the New Left, since that same new left makes every use of violence (in fact mirrors the violence) of the old Right. It is perfectly common to see those who protest American-supported atrocities in Central America address their legitimate grievances with the same violent rhetoric one hears issued from the White House. Hannah Arendt divides the world into those who hear the time-bomb ticking and those who do not. The "one of letters" who both supports and is dependent on the academies (and this includes myself), which are themselves dependent upon the business of violence, may make no legitimate claim to living a life of nonviolence.

Where I live is irretrievably bound up in how I live; and the "where" and "how" of a life define the life itself When Marx borrowed Hegel's notion of the seed of rebirth (revolution) being found in every society just as it is found in every living organism, he was exercising an optimism that is not often available to those born into a Nuclear Age. And yet the seed remains, just as surely as the final solution remains, 40 minutes down the road, ticking, ticking . . .

* * *

While we enjoy the creature comforts made possible by the suffering of those who came before us, we also inhabit the hells they created. The "one of letters" should be aware that a mid-sized paper mill fouls as much potable water in a single day as does the entire population of France, and that it costs us more to dispose of the four billion tons of waste we create each year than we spend on schools and hospitals combined. We have delivered 300,000 tons of non-biodegradable DDT into the world's watertable, enough to destroy plankton (our primary source of oxygen for the entire planet) in a hundred thousand million cubic meters of water forever.

The Buddhist precept of "right livelihood" means "not killing." Nearly four hundred million automobiles pour lead into the air each day, and each automobile "consumes" as much oxygen as thirty humans. It costs about the same to construct a six-lane freeway as it would to provide an electric train for the same route, and the train will deliver thirty times the number of passengers with only a fraction of the number of accidental deaths. But we have chosen our privacy over the quality of life for future generations. Partly, presumably, because we have little faith that there will *be* future generations.

We must come to the startling realization that a nation is nothing but an enormous commercial enterprise poisoned by patriotism, as Jerome Deshusses made clear in his astonishing study, *The Eighth Night of Creation*, and that a purely materialistic economics rooted in the idea of a "balance of trade" means that each country, in order to prosper, must export more than it imports, and that "the prosperity of one half of the world depends directly on the deficit [and suffering] of the other half . . ."

But it is impossible to live without producing waste. It is impossible to live without "technology." Right livelihood, right thinking, and right action are therefore founded in questioning the most basic assumptions about life in a technocratic state. Pseudo-"science" is not a suitable substitute for religion any more than the accumulation of "goods" is a substitute for being conscious.

Driving past the Hanford Nuclear Site, driving through the "Red Zone," driving down Hood Canal past the Trident nuclear submarine base as I head for my prison writing classes, I cannot help but think that our proclivity for technologizing and institutionalizing violence is nothing more than a feeble attempt to remove the human element from our incessant struggle to satisfy an obsessive and insatiable greed. And all the while, we continue to stockpile death, lying ourselves into believing we are other than the merchants of death, and that we build these weapons as a "deterrent" to war, knowing full well that humanity has made use of *every* weapon ever invented, no matter how unspeakably terrible the consequences.

And later, having returned past the same evil reminders, I walk out through the woods into the clear-cut, and I note each month's developments, how the whole process of reforestation relieves the wounds and scars we give the world. And I believe that it is not too late. It *is* late. But it may not be too late to begin a new life, one with its roots in human dignity, one with its roots in compassionate action and compassionate economics. And I remember the face of my friend who leads the struggle locally against domestic violence, how she looked at me and asked, "How can you spend so much time with those batterers, those sick, violent men?" And I remember particular faces from my prison writing classes, how certain of these men pay and pay with the memory of their cruelties, and how they begin to learn that cruelty is only a sick man's reaction to fear. And if I who have lived by violence cannot love them and remain unafraid, who will show them that fear is nothing and that our most precious commodity is hope and that without hope there can be no love in the world?

I do not hope to change the world. I do not hope to save us from ourselves. I do not even dare to hope that my poems will be of any use to other generations. Poetry does not exist in materialistic culture because poetry is a commerce of the spirit.

During my journey through this world, I hope to live a fruitful life, a life of nonviolence, a life of charity. I want to know that I have made choices, and I want those choices to be realistic. When I think of Basho's travels three years from now (if we *have* a life three years from now), I will remember that he inhabited the real world, and that he, too, felt that sense of *mono no aware*, and set out on his journey with compassion in his heart. In three years I will be forty-six years old and turning forty-seven, the same age as Matsuo Basho when he began his last, greatest journey. And I will hope against odds that my own greatest journey will still remain ahead. And if there is to be a journey for the soul, and if the journey of a thousand miles indeed begins with a single step, I begin mine here. Now.

Robert Wrigley

Photo by Barry Krough

ROBERT WRIGLEY was born in the Midwest and has lived for the last decade in Lewiston, Idaho, where he is Associate Professor of English at Lewis-Clark State College. His poems have brought him a number of awards, including fellowships from the National Endowment for the Arts, the Idaho Commission on the Arts, and the 1985 Celia B. Wagner Award from the Poetry Society of America. In 1986, Governor John Evans appointed him to serve as Idaho's Writer in Residence. His most recent book of poems, *Moon in a Mason Jar*, was published by the University of Illinois Press.

The Swing, the Snow, the Skull of a Hare

The old elm tree in my grandparents' front yard was gigantic. Never pruned, never shaded by taller trees, it must have grown with a fury and recklessness positively joyful, by tree-standards. My grandfather hung a swing from one of its lower, great-girthed spars, and watched his grandchildren swing as he sat on the front porch and swatted flies and popped cats with a BB-gun and read, word for trivial word, masthead to last want ad, every day's St. Louis *Post-Dispatch*.

The swing was wonderful. The chains that held it were at least fifteen feet long, and it took a good while to pump to that height at which the stomach lurches and swoops. At the far forward end of the ride, I was nearly out over Johnson Avenue, and now and then the rare passersby would look up startled at some squealing, gap-toothed, spindle-legged, bare-footed bird of a kid.

I played a lot of baseball and built forts in the woods and dammed the little filthy drainage creeks that ran there and climbed the local slag heaps and called them mountains, but I remember myself more often – and more vividly – in that swing than at any other sort of play. That plummet and rise, that wind made of speed and air, that pendulous, over-turned arc, was the motion of my childhood, the pulse of my summer days.

* * *

It must have been my fourth-grade teacher who made me memorize Frost's "Stopping By Woods on a Snowy Evening." I'm not sure anymore, though the poem is etched neatly – tattooed, even – on my memory. That summer, after fourth-grade I guess, I remember swinging, and I remember how the poem kept coming into my mind's ear. Two long syllables up, two more back. "Whose woods," I heard, and I was leaning back, pulling at the chains, stretching my legs outward for height; "these are," and I leaned my shoulders into the chains and tucked my legs below me. "I think . . . I know."

The motions of that swing taught me the neat discipline of

Frost's tetrameter. Sixty-four ups and backs, sixty-four swings in four impeccable quatrains. Two or three years ago, when my son was still young enough to enjoy swinging and not be embarrassed by it, I took him to a park here in Lewiston, Idaho. We could swing and look out over Tammany Canyon to the Blue Mountains of Washington and Oregon and to the low timbered, snow-belt hills known as Waha, and it all came back to me, swing after swing, line after line.

* * *

I am not at all ashamed to admit that I was drawn to the Northwest, and to Idaho, by geography. After more than twenty-five years in the farm-flat midwest, these mountains and canyons, these wild, far-falling rivers were, and are, exhilarating to me. That afternoon as my son and I swung, side by side so that we could talk and point and see together, I was struck as I am again and again by the beauty of this irregular landscape, this dramatic unlevelness. It appeals to me, I think, for the same reasons swinging did when I was a child. It is up and down, it is rhythm on a dazzlingly vast scale. It is not the reportorial, textbook-bloodless prose of plains and plains and plains; it's the bump and clatter of Hopkins, the exuberant dance of Roethke, the heartfelt limp and eloquent stagger that goes perfectly on in Hugo.

I think that we are all regional writers, that we all carry with us the landscape we have come to call home. Who can fail to see New York in Ashbery's prosody, or the woods of far western Washington in Wagoner's gorgeous, fog-scrimmed lines? When I write a poem, I mean for it to swing—less regularly, less liltingly than "Stopping By Woods on a Snowy Evening," perhaps; I mean for it to have the plummet and rise of the Northwestern landscape, the humps and canyons in its consonants, the wind-driven, river-borne music in its vowels.

That's what I shoot for anyway. Dull, conversational lines bore me. They are fallow fields in depressingly vast prairies; I love mountains, canyons, violent energy. "The Harsh Country," wrote Roethke, is "the country of ourselves." Dick Hugo liked to joke that people, in their scarcity, became more valuable here. "If you meet a person," he would say, "who has even one *remotely* redeemable characteristic, you make him a friend for life." This is a land in which people turn to and upon themselves, for lack of alternative, or for ulterior motive. The result in some cases is despair and madness; in others it is art. "That girl upstream was diced by scaling knives – / scattered in the shack I licked her knees in." Hugo's music is a schematic diagram as readable as a topographical map – harsh, powerful, and lovely.

* * *

And then there is that emptiness. It's not really like Hugo's joke, but it's not that far from it either. In Idaho, a gathering of 200 people constitutes a frighteningly large mob. There's a county in north central Idaho – Idaho County – in which deer and elk outnumber people, and which would hold, with room to spare, the states of Massachusetts, Connecticut and Rhode Island.

The effect of such a sparse population on a writer is hard – maybe even impossible – to figure. A dedicated minority works hard to generate cultural activities, but it's a thankless and frustrating task. Except for Missoula, over the mountains in Montana, there's nothing like a "literary center."

For me, the emptiness is comforting and exciting, but more than this, it's . . . well, conducive. On a hike, at a camp deep in the roadless country, the "wilderness," there is an exquisite melancholy that often comes over me. It's the same melancholy I feel when I listen to Samuel Barber's "Adagio for Strings" or Billie Holiday singing "God Bless the Child"; it's the same melancholy I feel when I read "Adam's Curse" or "Skunk Hour" or "Degrees of Gray in Philipsburg." A reasonable and predictable reaction, it is very likely what we feel in the face of what is great, in the presence of what is somehow larger than ourselves.

A poet, feeling this way, will inevitably write. Yes, the harsh, empty country is the country of ourselves, and the harsh empty landscape of Idaho (or of Montana and of much of Oregon and Washington) is a resource of immeasurable value. It has the roominess of all the imagination and the solitary emptiness of the self.

* * *

This past winter came early, heavy snows in November, good skiing before Thanksgiving. My wife and son and I borrowed a friend's cabin in the mountains near where we live and spent the better part of our Thanksgiving holiday there. One morning I got up early to stoke the fire in the wood stove; it was 28 degrees in the cabin. I perked a pot of coffee, left it to settle, and slipped into my skis for a trip through the woods and up onto a flat-topped knoll cleared some years ago by a forest fire. From on top you can see across Hells Canyon, with the Seven Devils Mountains on one side and the Oregon Wallowas on the other. The sky was clear; it would be a gorgeous—and frigid—dawn.

I made my way across a little creek and then upward through the trees and onto an old narrow gauge railroad bed, the last remnants of a logging operation sixty or seventy years in the past. I was hurrying; I wanted to make the ridge before the sunrise, but it was nearly dark there, especially so in the trees, and soon I was wheezing from the exertion and the altitude, and so I stopped.

The air was absolutely still. A little light had begun to sift down through the snow-laden timber. I thought to myself how in the seventy or eighty square miles of this little mountain range there were likely no more than six or seven people, and all of us had gotten here on skis or snowmobiles; there were no plowed roads here this time of year. It was that feeling, that exquisite melancholy, that silent, still exhilaration that the earth, and art, can bring on.

The day was lightening rapidly then. I knew I'd gotten too late a start, that I'd missed the sunrise, that there was coffee and warmth waiting for me back at the cabin, so I turned around and began to go. Just ten yards back I saw what, in the earlier darkness, I'd missed: the tracks of a snowshoe hare. Such tracks are nothing unusual; the hares are probably the winter's busiest travelers in the mountains. If you ski a mile, you'll see the tracks of several, or of one with a taste for meandering.

But I was already thinking of poems. I knew when I turned around there in the trees that my tablet and pens were on the table where I'd left them the night before. And at the moment I saw the tracks of the hare, I thought of the summer before, when my son and I, camping in another range of mountains not far from where I skied, found—intact—the skull of such a hare. We took it home and boiled it in bleach and used a dentist's pick to remove the last bits of flesh and hide. Now the skull was at home, on the dresser in my son's room, one of his most prized possessions.

> The Skull of a Snowshoe Hare
>
> I found it in the woods, moss-mottled,
> hung at the jaws by a filament

of leathery flesh. We have painted it
with chlorox, bleached it
in that chemical sun, boiled loose
the last tatters of tissue,
and made of it an heirloom,
a trophy, a thing that lasts, death's
little emissary to an eight-year-old boy.

What should it mean to us now
in its moon-white vigil on the desk?
Light from the hallway makes it loom
puffball brilliant, and I look.
For no good reason but longing
I am here in your room,
straightening the covers, moving a toy,
and lightly stroking your head,
those actions I have learned to live by.

If we relish the artifacts of death,
it's for a sign that life goes on
without us. On the mountain snows
we've seen the hare's limited hieroglyphics,
his signature again and again
where we've skied. And surely
he has paused at our long tracks there,
huddled still as moonlight, and tested
for our scents long vanished in that air.

We live and die in what we have left.
For all the moon glow of that bone
no bigger than your fist, there is more
light in the way I touch you
when you're sleeping: the little electric sparks
your woolen blankets make together,
the shape of your head clear
to my hand in the half-light,
and this page, white as my bones, and alive.

It is a quieter poem than usual. Blame that on the tenderness of the subject, the landscape softened under snow.

* * *

Later that same day we did make it up onto the ridge. We worked up a sweat in the climb, then sat in the sun on a cleared-off fallen tree and ate our lunch. The ski back to the cabin was the best part, though. The snow was perfect and fast. There were quick turns to be made and wonderful dips and downhills. Each of us took at least one great crash and laughed as we shivered and shook the snow out of our ears and shirts. That evening we tired early, my wife and son turned in, and I was the last one up, banking the stove, turning off the gas lights.

I stepped out onto the porch. It had clouded up quickly, as it will do in the mountains, and now a steady, windless snow was falling. I couldn't bring myself to go back inside. The silence was there again, colossal and endless. It was warmer than it had been earlier in the day, and so I stood, my hands in my pockets, and looked into the near darkness, and watched the woods fill up with snow.

Authors' Works

Deemer, Charles
    Plays Produced (date indicates first production)

Above the Fire, 1970.

The Dragon, 1971.

The Flooding of West Rapids, 1971.

The Profession, 1971.

The Battle of the Ages, 1976.

The Pardon, 1979.

Ramblin', 1979.

1934: Blood & Roses, 1980.

Mongrel Woman's Blues, 1981.

The Ballad of Sam Crab, 1981.

Country Northwestern, 1981.

The Half-Life Conspiracy, 1983.

Testing, 1983.

Christmas at the Juniper Tavern, 1984.

The Comedian in Spite of Himself, 1984.

Armed in the Spirit, 1984.

The Genie in the Bottle, 1984.

Echoes of the Peaceful Heart, 1985.

Abigail and Harvey, 1985.

Waitresses, 1985.

Abigail, 1986.

Chateau de Mort, 1986.

The Trouble with Wally, 1986.

    Plays Published

Christmas at the Juniper Tavern, Arrowood Books, 1985.

    Screenplays

Deadly Waters, Tom Shaw Productions, 1986.

    Videoplays

Granddaddy Tales: The Cowboy Who Couldn't Sing, John Mincey Productions, 1986.

Defrees, Madeline
>Nonfiction

The Springs of Silence, Prentice-Hall, 1953.
Later Thoughts from the Springs of Silence, Bobbs-Merrill, 1962.
>Poetry

From the Darkroom, Bobbs-Merrill, 1964.
When Sky Lets Go, George Braziller, Inc., 1978.
Imaginary Ancestors, CutBank/SmokeRoot Press, 1978.
Magpie on the Gallows, Copper Canyon Press, 1982.

Gale, Vi
>Poetry

Several Houses, Alan Swallow (New Poetry Series), 1959.
Love Always, Alan Swallow, 1965.
Nineteen Ing Poems, Press-22, 1970.
Clouded Sea, Press-22, 1972.
Clearwater, Swallow Press, Inc., 1974.
Odd Flowers & Short-Eared Owls, Prescott Street Press, 1984.

Gallagher, Tess
>Poetry

Stepping Outside, Penumbra Press, 1974.
Instructions to the Double, The Graywolf Press, 1976.
Portable Kisses, Sea Pen Press, 1978.
Under Stars, The Graywolf Press, 1978.
Willingly, The Graywolf Press, 1984.
>Fiction

The Lover of Horses, Harper and Row, 1986.
>Essays

A Concert of Tenses, Univ. of Michigan Press, 1986.
>Screenplays

Dostoevsky, (with Raymond Carver), Capra Press, 1986.

Halperin, Mark
>Poetry

Backroads, Univ. of Pittsburgh Press, 1976.
The White Coverlet, Jawbone Press, 1979.

Gomer, Sea Pen Press, 1979.

A Place Made Fast, Copper Canyon Press, 1982.

Hamill, Sam

Poetry

Heroes of the Teton Mythos, Copper Canyon Press, 1973.

Petroglyphs, Carnegie-Mellon Univ. Press, 1976.

The Calling Across Forever, Copper Canyon Press, 1976.

The Book of Elegiac Geography, Bookstore Press, 1978.

Triada, Copper Canyon Press, 1978.

animae, Copper Canyon Press, 1980.

Fatal Pleasure, Breitenbush Books, 1984.

The Nootka Rose, Breitenbush Books, 1987.

Translations

Night Traveling (from Chinese), Turkey Press, 1985.

The Lotus Lovers (from Chinese), Coffeehouse Press, 1985.

The Same Sea in Us All (from the Estonian of Jaan Kaplinski), Breitenbush Books, 1985.

Lu Chi's Wen Fu (The Art of Writing), Barbarian Press, 1986.

Catullus Redivivus (Selected Poems from Catullus), Blue Begonia Press, 1986.

Facing the Snow (Visions of Tu Fu), Barbarian Press, 1987.

Banished Immortal (Visions of Li T'ai-po), forthcoming.

Essays and Criticism

At Home in the World, Jawbone Press, 1981.

The Poetry of Kenneth Rexroth, Univ. of Michigan Press, forthcoming.

Hoyt, Richard

Fiction

Decoys, a John Denson mystery, M. Evans, 1980. Paper edition: Penguin Books, 1984.

30 for a Harry, a John Denson mystery, M. Evans, 1981. Paper edition: Penguin Books, 1984.

The Manna Enzyme, William Morrow, 1982.

Trotsky's Run, William Morrow, 1982. Paper edition: Tor Books, 1983.

The Siskiyou Two-Step, a John Denson mystery, William Morrow, 1983. Paper edition: as *Siskiyou*, Tor Books, 1984.

Cool Runnings, The Viking Press, 1984. Paper edition: Tor Books, 1985.

Fish Story, a John Denson mystery, The Viking Press, 1985.
Paper edition: Tor Books, 1986.
Head of State, Tor Books, 1985 (both hardcover and paper).
The Dragon Portfolio, Tor Books, 1986 (both hardcover and paper).
Seige!, Tor Books, forthcoming.

Inada, Lawson Fusao
Poetry

Before the War: Poems as They Happened, William Morrow, 1971.
Three Northwest Poets: Drake, Inada, Lawder, Quixote Press, 1971.
The Budda Bandits Down Highway 99: Hongo, Inada, Lau, The Buddahead Press, 1979.

Anthologies (as editor)

AIIIEEEEE!, Doubleday, 1976.
THE BIG AIIIEEEEE!, Howard University Press, 1985.

Jensen, Laura
Poetry

After I Have Voted, Gemini Press, 1972.
Anxiety and Ashes, Penumbra Press, 1976.
Bad Boats, Ecco Press, 1977.
Tapwater, Graywolf Press, 1978.
The Story Makes Them Whole, Porch Publications, 1979.
Memory, Dragon Gate, Inc., 1982.
A Sky Empty of Orion, Meadow Press, 1985.
Shelter, Dragon Gate, Inc., 1985.

Kittredge, William
Fiction

The Van Gogh Field and Other Stories, Univ. of Missouri Press, 1978.
Cord, (with Steven Krauzer), Ballantine Books, 1982.
Cord: The Nevada War, (with Steven Krauzer), Ballantine Books, 1982.
Cord: Black Hills Duel, (with Steven Krauzer), Ballantine Books, 1983.
Cord: Gunman Winter, (with Steven Krauzer), Ballantine Books, 1983.
Cord: Hunt the Man Down, (with Steven Krauzer), Ballantine Books, 1984.
Cord: King of Colorado, (with Steven Krauzer), Ballantine Books, 1984.
We Are Not In This Together, The Graywolf Press, 1984.

Cord: Gunsmoke River, (with Steven Krauzer), Ballantine Books, 1985.
Cord: Paradise Valley, (with Steven Krauzer), Ballantine Books, 1986.
Cord: Brimstone Basin, (with Steven Krauzer), Ballantine Books, 1986.

    Anthologies (with co-editor Steven Krauzer)

Great Action Stories, New American Library, 1977.
The Great American Detective, New American Library, 1978.
Fiction into Film, Harper and Row, 1979.
Contemporary Western Fiction, TriQuarterly, 1980.

    Films

Heartland, (as script consultant and writer), Wilderness Women, Inc., 1979.

    Essays

Owning It All, The Graywolf Press, forthcoming.

Rutsala, Vern

    Poetry

The Window, Wesleyan Univ. Press, 1964.
Small Songs, Stone Wall Press, 1969.
The Harmful State, Best Cellar Press, 1971.
Laments, New Rivers Press, 1975.
The Journey Begins, Univ. of Georgia Press, 1976.
Paragraphs, Wesleyan Univ. Press, 1978.
The New Life, Trask House Books, 1978.
Walking Home from the Icehouse, Carnegie-Mellon Univ. Press, 1981.
The Mystery of Lost Shoes, Lynx House Press, 1985.
Backtracking, Story Line Press, 1985.
Ruined Cities, Carnegie-Mellon Univ. Press, 1987.

    Anthologies (as editor)

British Poetry 1972, The Baleen Press, 1972.

Wren, M.K.

    Fiction

Curiosity Didn't Kill the Cat, Doubleday and Co., 1973.
A Multitude of Sins, Doubleday and Co., 1975.
Oh, Bury Me Not, Doubleday and Co., 1976.
Nothing's Certain But Death, Doubleday and Co., 1978.
Seasons of Death, Doubleday and Co., 1981.

The Phoenix Legacy, a trilogy, Berkley Publishing Group, 1981.
Wake Up, Darlin' Corey, Doubleday and Co., 1984.

Wrigley, Robert
    Poetry
The Sinking of Clay City, Copper Canyon Press, 1979.
The Glow, Owl Creek Press, 1982.
Moon in a Mason Jar, University of Illinois Press, 1986.
In the Dark Pool, Confluence Press, forthcoming.